DESIGNING WITH NOTIONS

designed & created by

robin johnson

debbie crouse

heidi swapp

written by dan maryon

Over 150 ways to use notions
for Scrapbooking, Cardmaking,
Gifts & more...

The Sophisticated Scrapbook
An Imprint Of Autumn Leaves

"Designing with Notions" is the
second book in a series of books published
under the imprint "The Sophisticated Scrapbook,"
a division of Autumn Leaves.

PUBLISHER: Jeff Lam
DESIGN DIRECTOR: Robin Johnson
with the expert help of Leaf Baimbridge
PRODUCTION: Autumn Leaves Studios

WRITER: Dan Maryon

PHOTOGRAPHY: Rastar Digital Media
ART DIRECTOR: Robin Johnson
Photographers: Bruce Johnson
and Doug Orgill

For information about bulk sales
or promotional pricing, please contact
Josie Kinnear at Autumn Leaves:
1.800.588.6707

The Sophisticated Scrapbook
A Division of Autumn Leaves,
Encino, California

PRINTED IN CANADA

DEDICATION

This book is dedicated to two groups

of people. First of all, our

families

Our husbands and children

have given up so much to help

make this book possible.

We express our great love for them.

We would also like to dedicate

this book to

you

We love creative people!

We thought of you as we planned and

worked on the book and hope it

will inspire you to create

wonderful things!

Best Wishes...

from Robin, Debbie and Heidi

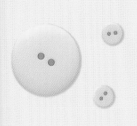

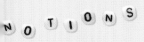

welcome

As we were working on this book,
our main objective was to come up with
fresh ideas and concepts that you could combine
on any page, with any topic to create effective
and interesting pages. Note the word:

concepts

Instead of considering this an
"idea" book, we would rather you
think of it as a CONCEPT book.

As you look at a page or card that you like, we
encourage you to break it down and determine
what it is that draws you to it.

Is it the color or texture combinations?
Is it the way things are laid out on a page?
Is it the way the photos are attached?
Do you like the way the journaling is
presented or the title is placed?
Do you like the lettering style?

Once you have identified the CONCEPT you like,
translate it to use with the photos you are working
with. For example, notice how this same concept is
used: On page 10, on "Alex Alexandra" Heidi criss-
crossed the hemp twine on the photo; Robin uses
the same concept on "Winter" on page 21,
this time done with fibers.

Some pages have one CONCEPT on its own,
others are a mixture of several small concepts.
Again, the idea is to break it down and determine
what you like, and how that can be used to your
advantage with your photos and memories!

This book was intended to be a teaching tool
so we chose to include as many instructions
and tips as possible so that you can easily see
how we did what we did.

We encourage you to take the CONCEPTS we
have shown and build from them. There is, of course,

no limit

to what you can do with any of these notions!
Our goal as scrapbook artists is to inspire you and
energize you, so you will take your art to the
next level!

contents

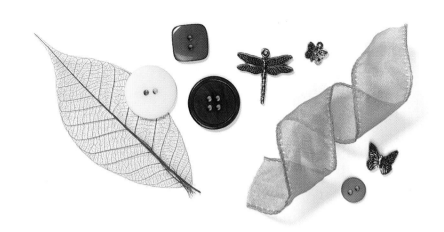

adhesives

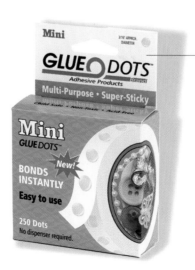

The term "notions" has been used very loosely in this book. The things we have decided to highlight don't easily fit into just one category! Notions seemed to portray the "little extras" and that is what these chapters are about: adding the little extras that make your project a unique piece of art.

The amount of product available to use in our scrapbooking craft making, card and book projects is unbelievable. Each one of them has a different type of surface to work with. Some types of product are glass, metal, wood, paper, or organic. The adhesives we use in scrapbooking, may not cover the variety of needs for these new products. In an effort to help you get started, we chose some of our favorite adhesives to work with and we'll tell you when we _____ use them most.

tip:

organization

One key to success when working with notions is to keep them organized. These products from Dritz are easy to use because of the clear lid on each container. You can use sewing boxes, hardware boxes, fishing boxes, metal containers such as this, or anything that has a lot of small compartments. Have one box for beads, one for buttons, one for brads and studs, etc. You'll love the freedom it gives you and the time that you'll save being organized.

E6000®
Aleene's Tacky Glue©

These adhesives both work well when you want to adhere bulkier items. Both are very thick and dry relatively fast and clear. The Tacky Glue [DUNCAN] is made with a small point for easy application. E6000 [ECLECTIC] comes with an extra tip that can be attached when needing a small amount of glue. Both are perfect for hard to hold items such as glass marbles, wood, hinges and metal objects.

Mono Multi®
Duo Embellishing Adhesive

Mono Multi [TOMBOW] is a favorite glue for paper to paper situations. It dries quickly and application is easy with one of the two different tip sizes. This glue is best used for things such as shadow boxes, when you need to adhere cardstock to foam board. It does dry clear, but leaves a little shine.

Duo Embellishing Adhesive [ART QUEST] is great for adhering light weight embellishments like glitter, microbeads, sequins, feathers, and especially gold leaf/foil flakes. You apply it with a thin and even coat and allow to dry just until tacky. Then place your items.

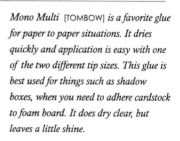

Glue Dots©

Glue Dots [GLUE DOTS] are a great alternative to liquid glues. The double-sided sticky dots are all archival quality. They adhere to a variety of materials including paper, plastic, wood, foam and more. There are different sizes for your various needs: Minis are great for small objects (sequins or beads), Memory Book dots are perfect for paper needs, Pop Up dots are 1/8" thick and create a 3-D effect. The possibilities are endless with this product.

tools

wire cutters
pliers

These two are essentials if you work much with wire or metals. The wire cutters [FISKARS] are great for thin sheet metal or mesh metal. They are also perfect for cutting all sizes of wire.

The pliers [MAKING MEMORIES] are helpful for working with wire. You can curl it, bend it or simply hold on to it with the pliers. They are also a great tool for strings and things that need to be pulled through holes, glued or tied.

Working with notions can be a lot easier when you have the right tool for the job. As we have worked on the book, these are some of the tools that we found to be most helpful.

There are many more great tools on the market to choose from! A variety like this will be a great place to start.

hammer
eyelet setter
anywhere punch

If you want to use eyelets, these tools are essential. The hammer [MAKING MEMORIES] is a great size for all your scrapbooking or paper arts needs.

The eyelet setter [CREATIVE IMPRESSIONS] is perfect for eyelets of all sizes. With the tapered point, it can do 1/16" eyelets too.

The anywhere punch [MAKING MEMORIES] allow you to set holes anywhere on your page, and the changeable heads allows you to punch a variety of sizes.

micro brush
glue brush
coloring tool

The micro brush [MAGIC SCRAPS] is made for precise application of adhesives, paints or solvents.

This multi-purpose brush [MAGIC SCRAPS] will actually work for applying adhesives or for guiding glitter as you work with it.

The coloring tool [TSUKINEKO] is brilliant for coloring with chalks. With a variety of point styles, you can pick the one that is just right for your project.

punch pick
paper piercer
needles

Needles [DRITZ] are basic for every scrapbooking tool kit. Use them for embroidery, beading, or for stitching on your pages. A variety of sizes will ensure that you have the right needle for the job.

The punch pick [MAGIC SCRAPS] is helpful for keeping your other tools in good shape. It can clear paper from your anywhere hole punch, keep glue tips clear, and work for a variety of other uses.

The paper piercer [MAKING MEMORIES] is a wonderful tool to have on hand. It can make holes in your paper for stitching, wire, fibers or other strings

x-acto knife
stylus (embossing tool)
tweezers

X-acto knives [PRO-ART] are another essential. A metal straight edge and an x-acto are great for cutting things like foam core, matte boards, even fabric. An inexpensive whole sheet of white matte board can be a great covering and cutting area on your desk.

A stylus or embossing tool [PLAID] is needed when dry embossing, but can also be used to score paper. This makes a nice, clean fold when creating books, envelopes, etc.

Tweezers [MAKING MEMORIES] can be helpful when you are working with small objects. The reverse action handle holds on to your piece for you. It also works well for holding objects while you apply the adhesive.

1 beads

Beads of all kinds make a playful addition to scrapbook pages, cards, and other crafts.

When you have a border or series of beaded strings, as on "Alyssa's Birthday," pierce holes in the card stock before you string the beads. Doing this helps you line up the stitching evenly and makes it easier to string beads on thread or wire.

For a beaded frame, as on "Pink Sunhat," mount the photo on card stock. With a needle, pierce two holes in each corner. Bring the wire up through one corner, add beads for the length of one side of the photo, then thread the wire through the first hole of the opposite corner. Bring the wire back up through the second hole, then wrap the wire once around the beaded portion before adding more beads.

HOW TO

This is a quick and easy gift or brag book. The album has a window in it, so I punched a square of ivory card stock to fit inside. I threaded the beads on wire, formed a circle and twisted the ends together, then tied the ribbon bow around it and glued the bracelet to the square (gluing behind the bow).

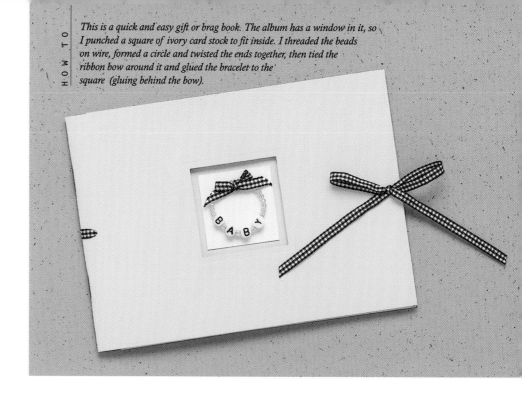

HOW TO

Use a bead for a flower center: Pierce a hole in the center of the flower and thread the wire or string up from the bottom. String the bead and thread back down through the hole. Twist the wire on the back of the paper (or tie a knot if using string). Use several beads for a larger flower.

The journaling block is stitched in place with the embroidery floss boxes around the flowers.

baby book
BY DEBBIE CROUSE
Album: Kolo Vineyard
Beads: Michael's
Beading wire: Darice
Square punch: Family Treasures
Ribbon: Renaissance

pink sunhat
BY HEIDI SWAPP
Vellum: Paper Adventure
Square punch: Marvy
Embroidery floss: DMC
Pens: Zig Millennium
Pencil: Prismacolor
Seed beads: Westrim
Beads: Beads Galore
Wire: Craft-T

Quincy's Pink sunhat Kauai HAWAII

because baby Q was only 6 months old, her sun exposure had to be very limited! This cute pink hat was the only one available, but i am a sucker for pretty much anything PInK! this hat was huge on her and she barely "tolerated" it, but the wide brim provided the necessary coverage! she was totally mesmerized by the water and the sand... it was so fun to watch her d i s c o v e r y

alyssa's
f i r s t   b i r t h d a y

cassie went all out on this party at vitale's. She made
adorable pinwheels for favors. we Ate pizza and cupcakes
baked in ice cream cones. we swam and played with
Toys! Alyssa recieved Lots of books, A Rocking CHAIR
Hand pAinted by grammy, A Toy chest, A doll and much
more! iT was so FUN to Celebrate Her special Day!

H O W T O For the horizontal border, thread the beads along the floss and tie large knots
between beads to control the placement of the beads. For the vertical border,
pierce holes on both sides of the torn paper border, then stitch and add beads at
random. Make the criss-cross photo corners in the same way, poking four holes
on either side of each corner and then stitching X's with the floss.

H O W T O Use a die to cut an envelope out of vellum. Fold a sheet of card stock in
half, and adhere a square of different color card stock on the center of the
front side. Apply the sticker to the square. Use embroidery floss to string
beads across the corners.

H O W T O To make the beaded border, cut card stock to size, then lightly pencil a
guide line for stitching. Measure between beads to ensure even spacing.
For this block title, position the letter stencil and lightly rub the ink pad
over it several times to fill in the color. Then outline with a gray pen.

She was lovely and fair with a *heart*
that was pure. She went about the kingdom
doing good. She was adored by all...
especially mom & Dad.

halloween
1992

alyssa's birthday
BY ROBIN JOHNSON
Embroidery floss: DMC
Beads: Designs by Pamela
Pens: Zig Millennium
Pencil: Prismacolor

mums card
BY ROBIN JOHNSON
Vellum: Autumn Leaves
Stickers: Autumn Leaves
Beads: Designs by Pamela
Embroidery floss: DMC

princess anna
BY ROBIN JOHNSON
Card stock: Bazzill Basics
Embroidery floss: DMC
Beads: Designs by Pamela
Pens: Zig Brush
Stamp ink: Shadow Ink
Stencils: Deja Views Letters
(2" Spunky)

2 fabric

Fabric and paper are both treasures of color and texture. If you have fabric scraps on hand, try them with your scrapbook pages for added richness.

You can sew fabric to the page, but gluing works as well as long as you lay the glue down lightly and evenly. Try spray adhesive or even run it through a Xyron machine.

Try fraying the edge of the fabric and using the selvage edge for different textures.

Debbie's love notes card set shows how well paper and fabric can work together. Cranberry felt and various wool scraps, including flowers cut from an old sweater, combine with decorative stitching for homespun charm.

HOW TO

Adhere the photo to the card front. Cut the sheer fabric about 1/2" larger than the photo, then stitch the fabric in each corner with 3 ply metallic thread and a bead. Attach the clear vellum announcement on the inside with a gold stud.

graduation announcement
BY DEBBIE CROUSE
Thread, sheer fabric: Joann's Fabric
Beads, gold stud: Michael's
Envelope: Savoir-Faire Stationery

alex alexandra
BY HEIDI SWAPP
Punches: Marvy
Hemp twine: Westrim
Stamps: Personal Stamp Exchange
Ink: Tsukineko
Pen: Zig Millennium
Paper clips: Clipiola
Button: Hobby Lobby
Beads: Powder Cake

HOW TO

To create a "tied down" look, pierce holes on either side of the photo and thread twine across. Try tying the ends in front of the photo rather than on the back of the page.

The large gold button had a wire eyelet, so I broke it off with pliers and adhered the button with a glue dot.

christmas traditions
BY ROBIN JOHNSON
Paper: Bazzill Basics
Rotary fabric cutter: Fiskars
Waxed Linen: Darice
Pens: Zig Writer, Zig Brush
Buttons: Hillcreek Designs

love notes card set

BY DEBBIE CROUSE
Embroidery floss: DMC
Ribbon: Renaissance
Love stamp: That's All She Stamped
Parcel Post stamp: thrift store
Cranberry felt: Kunin
Cotton bag: Flower Valley
Key charm: Bead Galore International
Envelope charm: Ink It!
Letter stamps: Personal Stamp Exchange

H O W T O

For a charming, simple gift project, work with equal parts fabric and paper. The card case is made of cranberry felt edged with a running stitch, with a gray wool patch and heart charm.

On the cards, stitch patterns on fabric with a contrasting color embroidery thread, attach charms or beads, and sew or glue fabric onto the card stock.

The tiny cards are kept in a plain cotton bag stamped to resemble a U.S. Mail bag.

H O W T O

For a cold winter theme, thin fleece or felt adds a cozy touch behind photos and even on titles.
To cut these loose fabrics, use a rotary cutter with a straight edge as a guide, on a fabric-cutting surface.
Use adhesive pop-up dots behind buttons to raise them slightly and make a handy "hanger" for photos or journaling blocks.

Christmas 2001

TRADITIONS CHECKLIST

☑ Go see the lights at the temple
☑ Act out the nativity with cousins
☑ Decorate the giving tree
☑ Decorate our tree
☑ See the Nutcracker
☑ Read Polar Express
☑ Open one gift on Christmas Eve
☑ Go and visit Santa
☑ Put one envelope gift on the tree for Gaye
☑ Hang out the stockings
☑ Give gifts
☑ Give thanks!!!
☑ Give love away
☑ Service to others
☑ Celebrate the joy of His humble birth

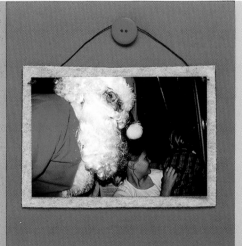

Our Christmas traditions are the same every year, but some of them were extra special this year!!

As we left Arizona, on December 19th, we took a detour to Williams, Arizona. There we boarded "the Polar Express" and got to ride to the North Pole!! When we arrived, Santa was there! The kids got to see him since he and Mrs. Clause rode the train back with us. They read the book, "The Polar Express" as we rode. It was wonderful!

We arrived in Utah just in time for the cousins Christmas party. Crissy got to be Mary this year in the play, and Lizzie and Sarah were beautiful angels. This is Grandma Pat's favorite tradition.

We also got to see the Nutcracker the day after Christmas. We saw it at Capitol Theater - the same place Mom saw it for the very first time when she was little.

3 charms

Small charms have a memorable, collectible style when combined with photos in a scrapbook. Attaching them is half of the fun: you can sew them on, tie them to hanging cords, use eyelets and wire, or dangle them from drop rings, fishing swivels, or similar hardware.

Heidi went all out with charms and small objects on "Kauai Memories," making a shadow box page filled with delightful bits of Hawaii.

Debbie's "Smile" card is perfectly simple. The unexpected camera charm does indeed raise a smile when the envelope is opened.

HOW TO

Die cut the outside envelope from a medium green. Trim off one side flap and turn sideways so the card can slide out (adhere the other flaps). Punch a 1 1/4" square in the back of the envelope; cut a square of darker card stock and punch a 3/4" square in it, then adhere to fit inside the larger square. Punch a 1/16" hole in the inner square and dangle the charm on a drop ring.

Cut a card from light card stock to fit inside the envelope. On the envelope flap, punch a 1/8" hole and fit an eyelet in it; the ribbon passes through the eyelet, around the back of the card inside the envelope, and comes out through a small slit cut in the edge of the envelope.

HOW TO

The photo block on the left is made with two small frames. Cut a piece of cardboard to fit inside each frame; for the bottom frame, adhere vellum on the cardboard and press inside the frame. Adhere the photo to the cardboard and press into the smaller frame, then adhere the smaller frame on top of the larger frame.

Ribbon does not need to stand out - notice how the green ribbon above and below the large photo is hardly noticeable but adds an elegant feel.

"smile" card
BY DEBBIE CROUSE
Punches: Family Treasures
Small hole punches: Fiskars
Envelope die: Ellison
Ribbon: Offray
Charm: Beads Galore Int.
Drop ring: Michael's
Eyelet: E-Z Set

maya's wedding
BY ROBIN JOHNSON
Vellum: Autumn Leaves
Ribbon: Offray
Charms: Creative Beginnings
Frames: Ink It!

let it snow
BY ROBIN JOHNSON
Paper: Bazzill Basics
Pens: Zig, EK Success
Charms: Michael's
Inks: Tsukineko
Stamps: Plaid Enterprises
Embossing Powder: Stamp-n-Stuff

kauai kemories
BY HEIDI SWAPP
Punches: Marvy
Pens: Zig Millennium
Stamp: Club Scrap
Letter stamps: Pixie
Inks: White Colorbox, Peerless Watercolors
Charms: Designs by Pamela
Glass puddles: Mega Marbles
Beads: Embellish It!
Brass wire: Westrim
Tags: American Tag
Paper clips: Clipiola
Other: Sand dollar, foam core, glitter glue

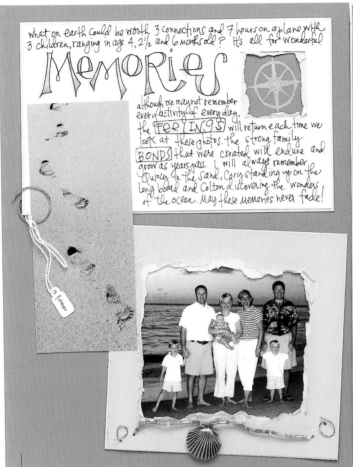

What on earth could be worth 3 connections and 7 hours on a plane with 3 children, ranging in age 4, 2½ and 6 months old? It's all for wonderful

MEMORIES

although we may not remember every activity of every day, the FEELINGS will return each time we look at these photos. the strong family BONDS that were created will endure and grow as years pass. I will always remember Quincy in the sand, Cory standing up on the long board and Colton discovering the wonders of the ocean. May these memories never fade!

HOW TO

For larger charms and notions, make a "shadow box" page: cut a frame from 1/4" foam core, then tear mattes from card stock in two colors and adhere on top of the foam core. The background of this page has varied colors painted with a simple watercolor wash, then seed beads are scattered on wet glitter glue for a beach pebble effect.

To dangle charms from the photos, place a tiny eyelet on the photo and attach the charm with thin wire.

HOW TO

Stamp the snowflake patterns and title words on the card stock, and while the ink is still wet, sprinkle embossing powder over the stamped designs. Shake off the excess powder and heat set it for a shiny, durable finish.

On the right page, notice how the white photo corners pick up the snowflake designs and also match the torn white matte behind the photo.

Since Lizzie was born & raised in Arizona, snow was a rare treat! Once we moved to Utah, it didn't take long before she could pack it like a pro!

Lizzie dec. '01

SNOW PASS

Unlimited Use
Unlimited Fun
Miles of Smiles

Let it SNOW   Let it SNOW   Let it SNOW

4 ribbon

There is such a variety of colors and textures available with ribbon, we could write an entire book on it. Ribbon is beautiful as a flat design element (for backgrounds and textures) and just as easily goes three-dimensional in any shape. A well-placed ribbon needs little else to accent a page.

Sheer ribbon can be used like vellum, to cover photos or other elements while still showing through. You can hold items in place with ribbon that is sewn to the page, such as the title and journaling blocks on "Desert Oasis." (Make sure the ribbon is just loose enough to allow items to slide in and out.) Or use a wide ribbon to form pockets by stitching it down on three sides.

desert oasis
BY HEIDI SWAPP
Punches: Family Tresures
Ribbon: Offray
Pencils: Prismacolor
Embossing powder:
Stamp-n-Stuff
Clips: Clipiola
Star studs: Memory Lane
Pop-up dots: Cut it Up
Fibers: Adornaments

collage card
BY ROBIN JOHNSON
Paper: Envelopments
Ribbon: MSI
Stamps: All Night Media
Inks: Tsukineko
Beads: Hirschberg Schutz & Co.
Fibers: On the Surface
Skeleton Leaf: Black Ink
Magic Mesh: Avant Card

HOW TO

To emphasize part of a photo, cut a square around the main interest (using an ultra large square punch). Adhere the photo background flat on the page, then adhere the square with pop-up dots to bring it forward. Loosely tie a decorative fiber around the photo square, and run a length of sheer ribbon behind the square but over the background. I used rust-colored embossing powder on the stars and the torn edge of the journaling block to give the page a desert-sand texture.

HOW TO

Run lengths of ribbons through a Xyron machine and adhere to the card stock. For textured ribbon, twist with wire so it holds its shape. Add magic mesh next, and color the mesh by "sponging" with ink pads. Add beads to the tag strings and tie to card through two small holes. Wrap fibers around card and tie, knotting fibers around the leaf stems.

princess

celebration

For Shelly & Kody's wedding, Tony wore a tuxedo, Cassie, a beautiful black silk dress and Alyssa was perfectly angelic in her darling white organza dress. They were truly a striking family! picture perfect... After the photos, Alyssa was escorted home by her grandparents for bed!

H O W   T O

The flowers are formed with ribbon, and leaves are cut from sheer green ribbon. To create your own ribbon roses, stitch the center down with your sewing machine. Rotate the card in a circular motion. and continue stitching as you go.

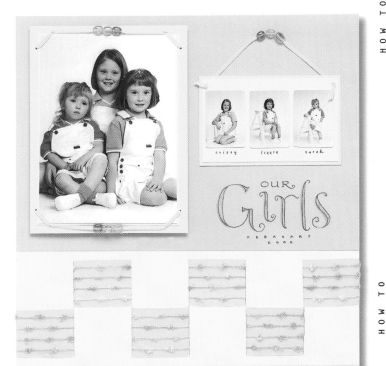

H O W   T O

Fold a sheet of card stock into thirds. On the left panel, punch mini holes for the flower petals, leaves, and stem. Use 1" sheer ribbon for the petals and 3/8" gold ribbon for the stem and leaves, and tape to the back of the paper. Glue a button flat to the paper and tie the jewelry tag around the stem. When the flower is complete, fold and adhere the left and center panels to hide the back of the flower. The right panel then becomes the inside of the card. Try using a scoring blade to get a smooth fold, especially if you are folding against the grain of the card stock.

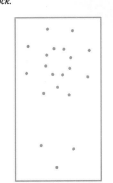

our girls
BY ROBIN JOHNSON
Card stock: SEI
Ribbon: Offray
Pencils: Prismacolor
Beads: Hirschberg
Schutz & Co.

vitale family
BY HEIDI SWAPP
Card stock: Bazzill Basics
Pens: Zig Millenium
Ribbon: Midori
Wood letter: Walnut
Hollow

ribbon flower card
BY DEBBI CROUSE
Ribbon: May Arts
Card stock: Bazzill Basics
Button: Old button box
Jewelry tag: American Tag
Adhesive: E6000

See Resources Section page 63

5 buttons

Buttons are a classic addition to many crafts. They add a homespun touch to pages that are formal or casual, and are a natural for baby pages or birth announcements.

Buttons are easily sewn onto card stock or other paper. You can also glue them down or tie them to twine or other fibers. Sometimes, what you adhere the button with can be just as interesting as the button itself.

grandpa bushman
BY ROBIN JOHNSON
Vellum: Autumn Leaves
Buttons: Hillcreek Designs
Pens: Zig, EK Success

will you marry me?
BY HEIDI SWAPP
Vellum: Autumn Leaves
Fibers: Fascinating Folds
Pencils: Prismacolor
Alphabet stamps: Pixie
Ink: Color Box
Silk ribbon: Bucilla Corp.
Jewelry tag: American Tag
Buttons: Old button box

I've never been so influenced by someone that I've never met...

GRANDPA BUSHMAN

HOW TO Wrap a thin strip of vellum around the journaling block and fasten with a button to make it look like a button closure. Cut the card stock mattes about an inch longer than needed, then fold over and tear the edge. Adhere buttons onto card stock. Although the fiber and ribbons tied through the buttons appear to be holding the button in place, you can tie them to the button and glue the button to the card stock just as easily. The fiber under the words "everlasting love" is simply glued to the page.

HOW TO Using wool fabric scraps and assorted buttons, stitch the fabric to the card stock or envelope using a straight stitch, running stitch, or X-stitch. Sew buttons on over the fabric.

everlasting LOVE

Remember the way this moment felt

Never let it fade

DREW ♥ TANIA

i love you...

will you marry me? & love me forever.

wrapped box
BY DEBBIE CROUSE
Printed paper: Memory Lane
Waxed linen: Darice
Button: Old button box

inspire button box
BY DEBBIE CROUSE
Tassle: Artifacts, Inc.
Box: Michael's
Adhesive: E6000 glue,
Modge podge
Buttons: Old button box
Other: Old dictionary

remember book
BY DEBBIE CROUSE
Filler paper: Strathmore
watercolor paper
Punch: C. S. Osborn & Co.
Stamps: Hero Arts, Stampa Rosa
Glassine envelope: Memory Lane
Adhesives: E6000 (tiles), Hermafix
Waxed linen: Darice
Tag: American Tag
Ink: Sandalwood
Buttons: Old
button box

button cards
BY DEBBIE CROUSE
Embroidery floss: DMC
Envelope: American Tag
Fabric scraps

HOW TO *Wrap a small gift with a nice printed paper, then cut a strip of card stock and wrap around the box. Tie it together with waxed linen, threading the button on the top and tying a knot.*

HOW TO *Paint the box with modge podge and smooth torn pages from an old dictionary around it. When dried, paint another coat of modge podge over the paper. Glue assorted buttons to the sides and top of the lid, adding a tassle or other decoration as desired.*

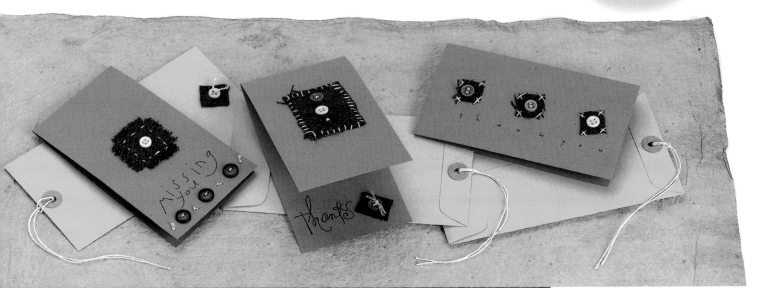

For the cover, cut a 12" x 12" sheet of kraft chipboard in half. Stamp designs on the front and back. Punch three 1/2" holes along the left side to bind the album. Tear watercolor paper to fit inside album and punch matching holes on the left of the pages. Bind with waxed linen, threading through buttons on both front and back. For the button closure, pierce a needle hole on both covers and sew button on front and back. Secure a 5" length of waxed linen to the back button, then wind around front button to close book.

HOW TO *To make the front cover open more easily, score the chipboard about 1/2" past the buttons on the left. I use the scoring blade in my Fiskars paper trimmer.*

6 nature

What is more evocative of a time and place than dried flowers or leaves? When properly dried and pressed flat, these bits of nature complement your pages or projects beautifully.

Remember to protect them in scrapbook pages, because they're not permanent. Use special acid-free pockets or glassine envelopes, or make your own protective coverings with page protectors. You might even try sticker makers for small, flat items.

Don't hesitate to use any number of natural accents. Robin's "Elements" matches abstract photos of natural beauty with twigs, a flat rock, and dried leaves.

HOW TO — *Lightly glue the leaf to a torn square of watercolor paper, and stamp over it with an embossing ink pad. Then sprinkle ultra thick embossing enamel over it, shake off the excess, and heat set the enamel. Stitch to card stock with waxed linen. Use a glue stick to adhere the torn dictionary definition to the card stock, then add more embossing enamel over it and heat set it.*

HOW TO — *Use special 4x6 photo pages for photos, journaling, or little treasures. Dried leaves will stay in position*

Use special 4x6 photo pages for photos, journaling, or little treasures. Dried leaves will stay in position with just a dab of glue on the card stock.

For journaling blocks, cut pieces of vellum and cardstock the same size, then cut a rectangle out of the cardstock to make a frame. Add adhesive under the cardstock so it doesn't show on the vellum. A dried leaf behind the vellum and a piece of twine wrapped around the frame make striking focal points.

Create your own tags with bits of card stock and 1/16" eyelets, with thin twine as a tie. Make a twine border for a photo by adding eyelets to each corner, then threading twine and knotting it around the corners.

See Resources Section page 63

OUR FIRST SUMMER WITH **uncle CLARK**

PLAYFUL

NATURE LOVER!

Throwing rocks in the river, motorcycle rides, the tree swing and bare back rides on the horses in the pasture are only a few of the wonderful adventures my kids dragged their NEW uncle clark along for! Katie and Clark were married in February and Colton and Cory quickly "broke him in" to his new-found unclehood! Clark's energy seemed boundless and his Love immediate toward my little ones! I will be always thankful for the quiet moments I was afforded by a generous and playful uncle clark! And down the road—I'll repay the favor! AUGUST 2001

grow card

BY DEBBIE CROUSE

Watercolor paper: Strathmore

Waxed linen: Darice

Clear embossing ink: Ranger

Embossing enamel: Suze

Weinberg's Ultra Thick

Adhesive: UHU glue stick

uncle clark

BY HEIDI SWAPP

Punch: Marvy Uchida

Hemp: Memory Lane

Pens: Zig Millennium

Ink: Adirondack Woodlands

by Ranger Industries

Alphabet stamps: Pixie Antique

Eyelets: E-Z Set

Tags: Avery

Embroidery floss: DMC

Photo holders: 20th Century

Products

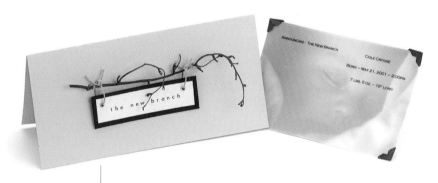

Try using small branches on cards. You can hang a "sign" from the branch as shown here, then tie the branch to the card with hemp twine.

For the card, print the announcement on vellum and trim to the photo size, then use photo corners to hold both in place.

If you clip the branches during the plant's growing season, you can press them lightly so they dry fairly flat. (Dry branches break too easily to flatten.)

HOW TO

elements

BY ROBIN JOHNSON

Corrugated card stock: DMD

Alphabet stamps: Personal

Stamp Exchange

Block Stamp: Stamper's

Anonymous

Wire: Artistic Limited Inc.

Chalk: Craf-T Products

the new branch

BY DEBBIE CROUSE

Vellum: Paper Adventures

Photo Corners: Canson

Hemp: Darice

Eyelets: EZ Set

grandma's ivy

BY ROBIN JOHNSON

Paper: Black Ink

Pens: Zig Brush, Zig Writer

Inks: Tsukineko ink

Stamps: Hero Arts,

Shadow Blocks

Adhesive: glue dots

Button: Dress It Up

HOW TO

The shadow block stamps behind the page title repeat the pattern of the bricks on Grandma's house without drawing too much attention.

7 wood

There are plenty of innovative wood shapes available in craft stores. Look for thin, light wood that can easily be glued to card stock or tied down on the page.

Unfinished wood looks great and takes no time at all. You can also apply inks, paints, and gold leaf to wood, which can be used in much the same way as paper.

One warning: wood contains lignin and the same elements that make paper acidic, so be careful about placing wood directly on photos. Use transparent protection, such as page protectors or other archival-quality plastic, between the wood and the photo.

cole box

BY DEBBIE CROUSE
Punch: Family Treasures
Stamps: Printworks,
Personal Stamp Exchange
Inks: Hero Arts Shadow Ink
(wheat, gold), Ancient Page (coal)
Adhesive: Modge Podge
Kraft box: Michael's
Wood discs: Michael's

See Resources Section page 63

HOW TO

Using a 1 7/8" kraft box, stamp letters on the box and lid. Try gold and wheat inks to "age" the lettering. Paint 1 1/2" wooden discs with black paint, then gently sand the edges to give them a worn look. Punch photo details out with a 1 1/4" circle punch, then apply to the discs with Modge Podge. Let dry, and apply one or two more coats on the front and back of the discs.

My grandson will sit for the longest time putting things in a box and taking them out again and again. He enjoys it even more with pictures of himself, and with these details of smiles, hands, and toes he can learn parts of the body as well.

HOW TO

To give letters and shapes a gold leaf look, apply adhesive with a brush and let it dry until tacky. Press on foil flakes and smooth over with a tissue or light cloth.

love

BY HEIDI SWAPP
Pens: Zig, EK Success
Pencils: Prismacolor
Chalks: Craf-T
Beads: Designs by Pamela
Fiber: "On the Surface"
Wood shapes & letters:
Walnut Hollow
Gold foil: Amy's Magic
Foil Flakes
Adhesive: Duo

We moved to Utah on December 15th — right in the middle of WINTER !! Chrissy loved playing in the snow — everthing from snowballs to snowmen & sledding.

WINTER

HOW TO

The miniature book is made with 1" square wood tiles and card stock pages made with a 7/8" punch. Use a 1/16" drill bit to drill three holes in the wood pieces, and punch tiny holes in each page. Lace together using waxed linen. Personalize your book with tiny pictures, fabric scraps, small punched shapes, vellum overlays, stamped or written words, envelopes, and anything else you can think of.

This book was put in a sheer bag and given as a Valentine's Day gift. It's not as hard as it may look!

winter
BY ROBIN JOHNSON
Card stock: Bazzill Basics
Twine: Memory Lane
Pens: Sakura
Photo corners: Canson
Eyelets: Coffee Break Design
Wood shapes: Darice

ten reasons i love you
BY DEBBIE CROUSE
Square punch: Family Treasures
Waxed linen: Darice
Stamps: Personal Stamp Exchange
Ink: Ancient Page
Tag: American Tag
Wood tiles: Darice

8 flowers

Dried flowers are a beautiful and treasured memory. Unfortunately, they are fragile and don't always last. Take care to protect them in scrapbook pages.

Plastic page protectors, vellum or glassine envelopes, and flat plastic boxes are used on these pages to hold flowers. Even a light sheet of acid-free tissue can help keep the flowers intact. If you plan to place flowers directly on photos, you should have some kind of acid-free protection between the two to avoid damaging the photo.

There are also new products available that preserve dried flowers in scrapbook friendly ways, such as stickers with real pressed flowers and leaves.

HOW TO

Die cut two cards, and cut one in half at the fold. This will be the inside frame piece. Trim 1/8" off each edge of the inside frame. Cut a clear sheet protector on the fold, sizing it 1/2" larger than the window on all sides. Place a dried flower inside the plastic sheets and glue the plastic together at the corners. Adhere inside frame to full card, and stamp a message on the front of the card.

This is a quick and easy way to make a card. You can go to your favorite scrapbooking store and die cut several cards in different colors to have on hand.

yellow flower card
BY DEBBIE CROUSE
Card die: Ellison
Stamp: Stampa Rosa Inc.
Stamp pad: Ancient Page
Sheet protector: Avery

purple flower card
BY ROBIN JOHNSON
Handmade paper: Black Ink
Flower: Hand pressed
Cardstock: Bazzill Basics

lizzie's blossoming
BY ROBIN JOHNSON
Letters: cut from K & Co. vellum
Twine: Hillcreek Designs
Flowers: Nature's Pressed
Tag: American Tag
Adhesive: glue dots

nature's beauty
BY HEIDI SWAPP
Vellum envelope
Punches: rectangle, square
Pens: Zig Millennium
Pencils: Prismacolor
Other: dried daisy, glitter glue

cousin country
BY ROBIN JOHNSON
Patterned paper: Doodlebug
Solid paper: Making Memories
Handmade paper: Black Ink
Buttons: Hillcreek Designs
Flowers: NuCentury
Eyelets: Creative Impressions
Embroidery floss: DMC
Other: green twine, waxed linen

Nature's
beauty

SUMMERtime
enchanted
alive
gARDEN
carefree
bAREFOOTED

remember
DiSCOVER
fragrant

freedom
EXPLORE
BLOOM
summertime
childhood

HOW TO

Stitch the top and bottom of the ribbon to lay it flat. Thin vellum word strips are lightly adhered over photos. Zig-zag stitch the torn photo to the page.

For the main journal block, cut or punch holes in the envelope and cut a piece of card stock to fit inside. Lightly mark the location of the holes on the card stock, then adhere photo to fit in one hole. Add journaling to card stock (showing through a hole or not) and the envelope itself. Behind the word "garden" a punched piece of vellum was adhered to the card stock to darken the green color.

COUSIN COUNTRY

lizzie and Sarah had so much fun playing with Hannah and Drue at Harvey's ranch. The fresh Wyoming air was wonderful for enjoying the great out doors. They laughed, played games, told secrets & had fun!

The sound of little girls laughter is a touch of heaven.

drue · hannah · lizzie · sarah

9 matte boards

Photo mattes of paper are the norm in scrapbooking, but why not try actual matte boards? They can give a more artistic look to the page and a solid feel you can't get with paper. You can also take advantage of their more sturdy weight to adhere or wrap fabric or other accents on them.

A store bought matte can provide a quick decoration, as on Robin's "Devin" page. You simply need to match other papers and notions to the colors of the matte.

Run leopard print paper through a Xyron machine and attach to matte board. Punch five holes on each side with an anywhere punch. Thread the elastic through the holes in straight and zig-zag lines.

TIP: I made this for my daughter's dorm room since she can't nail into the walls. It's light enough that it can be hung with sticky mounting tabs (the bulldog clips can hang it to the mounting hooks).

On this framed photo, the inside matte is touched up with magic gold leaf flakes and a gold charm is adhered to the outside matte. Beads are added just inside the matte. Two holes are pierced to the back of the page for each side of the photo. For the photo collage, adhere photo mounting sleeves to the page, then cut photos and word strips to fit. The photo sleeves are different widths and are overlapped to contrast the clean lines of the opposite page.

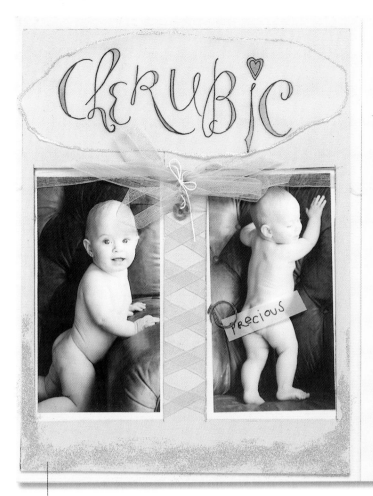

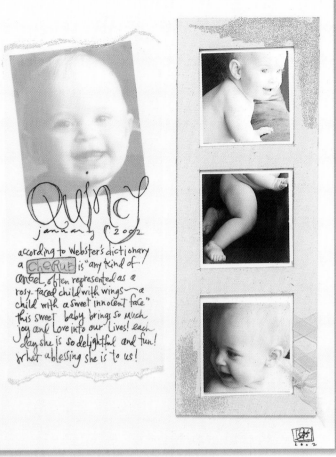

Cherubic

Quincy
january 2002

according to Webster's dictionary a CHERUB is "any kind of angel, often represented as a rosy-faced child with wings—a child with a sweet innocent face" this sweet baby brings so much joy and love into our lives! each day she is so delightful and fun! what a blessing she is to us!

precious

HOW TO

Cut the matte board to size, then use a straight edge and Xacto knife to cut holes for photos (draw a light pencil line as a guide). You may need several passes to cut through, depending on the thickness of the board. To add glitter to the title, tear the vellum and paint adhesive just on the edges. Allow the glue to dry until tacky, then sprinkle on glitter. To wrap ribbon around the matte, take a length of ribbon and hold the middle of the ribbon at the bottom. Wrap the right half of the ribbon all the way to the top, then wrap the left half, overlapping and crossing at the same angle. Tie a knot at the top to hold it firmly, then tie a bow. On this page, there are two bows to give more bulk to the ribbon

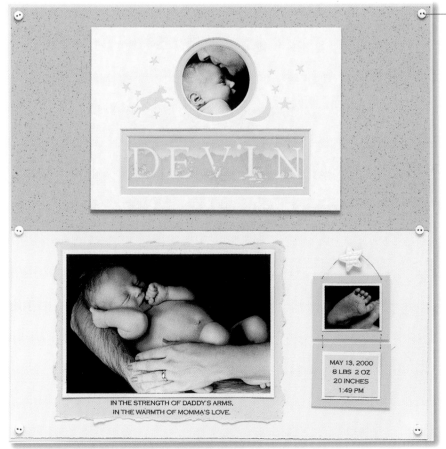

DEVIN

MAY 13, 2000
8 LBS 2 OZ
20 INCHES
1:49 PM

IN THE STRENGTH OF DADDY'S ARMS,
IN THE WARMTH OF MOMMA'S LOVE.

HOW TO

To create the mini-frame set, cut two pieces of matte board the same size. To make the holes for the wire, use a hammer and gently tap a large needle in the board where you want the hole to be. Pull the needle out and thread the wire through the holes.

M Board
BY DEBBIE CROUSE
Hole punch: Fiskars
Letter rubber stamp:
Hero Arts
Remember rubber stamp:
Stampa Rosa
Round elastic: JoAnne's
Clip: Clipiola
Tags: American Tag
Wood letter: Walnut House
Bulldog clips: OfficeMax
Adhesive: Xyron
Chalk

Cherubic
BY HEIDI SWAPP
Vellum: Paper Adventures
Square punch: Marvy
Ribbon: Bucilla
Embroidery Thread: DMC
Pens: Zig Millennium
Pencils: Prismacolor
Heart jewel: Crystal
Components
Adhesive: Duo glue
Other: Powder glitter
Clip: Clipiola

Sharing Secrets
BY HEIDI SWAPP
Crackle paper: Creative
Imaginations
Beads: Designs by Pamela
and Westrim
Matte board: Target
Doodle Mat
Gold leaf: Amy's Magical
Gold Leaf Flakes
Photo sleeves: Kolo
Gold studs: Dritz
Other: Velvet ribbon
and gold cording

Devin
BY ROBIN JOHNSON
Matte and sticker letters:
K & Company
Star button: Dress It Up
Buttons: Dress It Up
Wire: Westrim

10 envelopes & pockets

Envelopes and pockets, whether ready-made or hand cut with dies or patterns, make a perfect interactive touch for scrapbook pages or note cards.

For simple pockets, cut rectangles of paper and stitch or glue them to the page on three sides. A notch in the open end can make it easier to slip things in and out. Position a circle punch halfway over the edge to cut a half circle (as shown on "I Adore Him" and Debbie's garden party card).

Envelopes are perfect for storing notes, letters, extra photos, or memorabilia. Use an opaque envelope to conceal special letters and personal things. Try a sheer envelope when you want to display your wonderful treasures.

garden party card
BY DEBBIE CROUSE
Vellum: Autumn Leaves
Circle punches: Fiskars (1/8"),
Family Treasures (7/8")
Envelope die cut: Ellison
Ribbons: Dianne's
Gold leafing pen: Krylon
Adhesive (envelope):
3L Photo Tape

forever
BY HEIDI SWAPP
Thread: Hillcreek Designs
Label holder: woodworker.com
Pens: Zig, black and platinum
Charm: Boutiques Trims, Inc.
Gold Leaf: Amy's Magical
Gold Leaf Flakes
Clips: Clipiola
Ribbon: Bacilla

HOW TO

Die cut the envelope. Trim off one side flap, then seal the other sides with photo tape. Punch a half circle notch with a 7/8" punch. Print the invitation and trim to fit in envelope. Punch a 1/8" hole in center top and loop 1/8" ribbon through the hole. The card tied on front is made with two layers of card stock. The green layer has been edged with a gold leafing pen.

HOW TO

The vertical pocket is created by doing a blanket stitch around the outside perimeter of the pocket to the page. It is easier to stitch if you poke the holes first. To add color and flair, I added a strip of lighter color green paper to the inside edge of pocket and gold-leafed the torn edge. I mounted the label holder with grommets.

forever

To give the photo frame a rustic look, rub the paper edges with coarse sandpaper, then lightly shade with black chalk. The title block paper was first crumpled, then chalk was rubbed over the edges and added in to some of the letters.

There are many pre-printed accents that can be cut up to make cute pockets. To make tags for each pocket, cut a rectangle to size, notch the corners, and add an eyelet at the top. Next, add lettering with pen. Finally, apply chalk and rub into the paper.

HOW TO

i adore him
BY ROBIN JOHNSON
Card stock: Bazzill Basics
Circle punch: Carl
Die cuts: Fresh Cuts, EK Success
Eyelets: Magic Scraps
Waxed linen: Darice

heritage album
BY DEBBIE CROUSE
Watercolor paper: Strathmore
Punch: Anywhere Punch
Ribbon: Offray, Midori and Morex
Fabric: JoAnne's Fabric
Brass eyelets: Dritz

For album pages, tear ten sheets of watercolor paper to size. For the cover, cut two pieces of matte board that are 1/4" bigger than your inside paper. For the binding strip on the left front cover, cut a strip from one board about 1 3/8" wide. Cut 4 pieces of fabric 1/2" bigger on all sides than the back cover. Stitch ribbon pocket to fabric for front cover. Next, sew the fabric front sides together on three sides, turn right side out, then insert the large matte boards. Slip stitch the fourth side on the back cover. For the front cover, sew along the edge of the matte board to hold it in place. Next, insert the binding strip of matte board, then slip stitch the end.

Punch two 1/8" holes in both covers and all pages, and add eyelets in the holes on front and back cover. Thread the ribbon through from the back and tie a bow in front.

Make corner pockets on pages by stitching sheer ribbon to paper. Horizontal pockets are made with two layers of ribbon, the smaller one to hold picture labels or journaling blocks.

11 strings

String, twine, raffia, jute, twistel, thread, embroidery floss: anything you can use to tie, wrap, or keep things closed can be used to decorate a page or card.

Take advantage of the fluid lines you can get with fibers to make round, free spirited decorations. And learn to look at everyday materials in new ways. It's always fun to rediscover twine as, say, a photo border.

our english cottage
BY ROBIN JOHNSON
Handmade paper: Black Ink
Micro punch: Fiskars
Twistel: Making Memories
Paper flowers: Natural Paper Co.
Square stamp: Hero Arts
Alphabet stamp: Stampers Anon.
Ink: Tsukineko

boxed up
BY DEBBIE CROUSE
Vellum: Paper Adventures
Handmade paper: Black Ink
Punch: Family Treasures
Waxed linen: Darice
Hemp: Darice
Eyelets: Magic Scraps

wyoming round-up
BY ROBIN JOHNSON
Textured paper: Black Ink
Corrugated paper:
DMD Industries
Chalk: Versacolor
Eyelets: Dritz
Cord: Ben Franklin's
Pens: Zig

great kid
BY HEIDI SWAPP
Hemp: Michael's
Pens: Zig Millennium
Alphabet stamps: Personal
Stamp Exchange
Ink: Clearsnap Inc.
Tape measure: Dritz

HOW TO

Tear a piece of corrugated cardboard from a box, and tear the printed vellum to size it slightly smaller. Tie around both with waxed linen. If you like, lightly adhere the vellum to the cardboard with spray adhesive or glue stick.

The envelope is made with a custom pattern cut out of handmade paper. Adhere 1/2" circles of card stock to the flaps and attach eyelets in the center of the circles. Secure with hemp twine.

HOW TO

To make the flower stems, cut the desired length of twistel plus two inches more. Unravel the two extra inches and cut leaf shapes out of it. Punch a small hole with a micro punch at one end of each leaf and thread the stem through. Adhere the stems and leaves to the page, then add the paper flower.

Wyoming ROUND-UP

a Round-up of Cousins and Cows...

We had so much fun when we went to Harvey's ranch in May 2001. One afternoon we rounded up all the kids to take photos. There was quite a crew! We were so thankful that our kids have such great cousins! Later, we walked out the cabin to see this herd of cows! The cowboy was so neat to watch. He and his dog keep them all in line! It was better than the movies.

Sarah seemed to be working on a round-up of her own! She had daddy wrapped around her finger in no time at all! She's a sweetie.

HOW TO
For "wood" letters, cut narrow strips of corrugated paper. Shape into basic letters and adhere with glue dots. For "rope" lettering, shape cord into letters and put down small dots with a hot glue gun to hold it in place.

HOW TO
For a rough framed look, sew heavy twine or cord around the edges of photos. First, matte photos with paper (torn edges add extra dimension) and adhere to page. Cut lengths of cord to fit around edges of photos with a little to spare. With a zig-zag setting, stitch down the cord, using a 0 length setting at the beginning and end to secure the cord. Mix up your journaling by stamping key words in between written words.

ONE DAY i woke up and all of the sudden you weren't a baby anymore! You are growing up right before my eyes! each day you are more interested in the world around you. Constantly asking questions learning new things. Seems like i LOVE you more each day.

great kid
february 2002
newport beach

wire

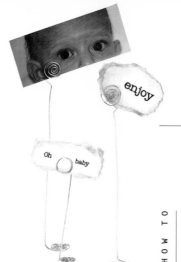

Lightweight artistic wire can be used in so many ways to add small touches to a scrapbook page. Fine wire can take the place of thread for beadwork or stitching, while heavier weights can be shaped as decoration or to hold items on the page.

There are many tools on the market for shaping wire. Take some time to explore these, and make sure you have the basics: needle-nosed pliers, wire cutters, and shaping tools. Of course, you can use anything from a heavy nail to a round marker barrel to shape wire.

all wired up
BY DEBBIE CROUSE
20 gauge silver wire:
the Beadery
Chalk pencils: Pixie Press
Font: Typist

blessing card
BY DEBBIE CROUSE
Cable, ring terminals: Home Depot
Jump rings: Michael's
Brads: Creative Impressions
Rubber stamp alphabets: Playful Alphabets by Hero Arts, PSX Celtic & Antique lowercase by Printworks

HOW TO

These are fun for something different to set on a desk or shelf. Using an 18" piece of wire start coiling one end until desired size. Coil other end for base and attach a picture or sentiment.

HOW TO

Cut a length of 16 gauge cable and crimp ring terminals onto ends. Attach ends to card with silver brads. Attach stamped squares to cable using jump rings. Buy cable by the foot from home improvement stores - it's very inexpensive! I couldn't find enough different shades of purple cardstock, so I used paint chips instead.

posies card
BY DEBBIE CROUSE
Silver wire: Michael's
Flowers & vase cut-outs:
Jolee's Boutique

hang in there card
BY DEBBIE CROUSE
Flower punch: Family Treasures
Embroidery floss: DMC
22 gauge silver wire: Michael's
Aluminum metal: Maid-o'Metal

happy day card
BY DEBBIE CROUSE
Ribbon: Offray
Silver wire: the Beadery

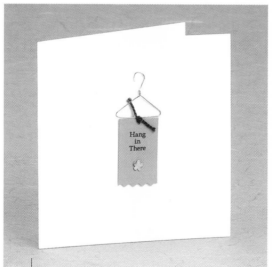

HOW TO

This is a fast and easy card with small cut-out shapes. Adhere the pre-made flowers and vase to the card. Curl one end of a 4" piece of 26 gauge wire and insert end of wire into vase. Attach word strip to curled wire. I made a whole page of small sentiment word strips for cards like this. Just print a number of thoughts, like "congratulations," "thank you," "get well," and "happy birthday" using a variety of fonts, then clip and use as needed.

HOW TO

To bend wire in a hanger shape, start in the middle of the wire and bend the two corners of the hanger around needle nose pliers. Twist the two ends together and trim one end off at the twist. Bend the other end around the pliers to form the hook. Punch a tiny hole in the note card and attach to hanger with embroidery floss. Adhere the note to the card, and add a tiny drop of glue to hold the hanger in place. This also works for "Let's hang out" or other card sentiments. You can also buy ready-made wire hangers from Jolee's Boutique.

HOW TO

Wrap 20 gauge wire evenly around a 1/2" diameter marker about ten times. Pull off the marker and carefully flatten wire on its side. Punch 1/8" holes in the card at top and bottom of where the wire is placed, and attach wire to card with two lengths of 1/8" ribbon. Tie ribbon to top of wire and wrap ribbon through the hole and around the top of the card. Repeat for bottom of wire. Insert picture and word strip between the wire circles.

just plain cute

BY ROBIN JOHNSON
Vellum: Autumn Leaves
Wire: Artistic Wire Ltd.
Tag: American Tag
Paper clips: Target
Eyelets: Dritz
Beads: Mill Hill,
Designs by Pamela

happily ever after

BY HEIDI SWAPP
Handmade paper: Black Ink
Rectangle punch: Family
Treasures
Copper wire: Artistic Wire
Dried flowers: Nature's Pressed
Purple leaves: Black Ink
Fiber: Ink It

HOW TO

To add beaded wire strips, cut wire 1" longer than needed. Bend 1/2" of one end at a 90 degree angle, then thread beads onto other end. When finished, bend 1/2" of other end. Pierce the paper with a needle and push the 1/2" ends of wire through, then bend to lay flat on back of page and secure with tape.

HOW TO

The handmade paper has small leaves, so I glued dried flowers and decorative leaves directly on the paper so it looks like they are pressed into the paper.

Journaling blocks and vellum strips are held in place with wire. Cut the wire twice as wide as the paper it will hold. Pierce the page with a needle and thread the wire through so one fourth of the length comes up through on both sides. Twist the wire on both ends into a spiral that lays flat against the page, and secure the paper strip in the spiral.

The wire can also run behind the photo. Bend the ends around the edges of the photo, and hold the wire in place with a strip of tape on the back of the photo. Twist the ends as above. Tie bits of fiber, or thread and beads, onto the wire.

mini-books

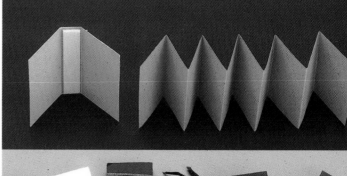

Handmade books are a charming way to present photos or send a memory album to someone. And they're so easy to make: cut paper to size, fold, and bind with cord.

For covers, an extra layer of paper gives a sturdier support. You can also try various kinds of bindings for thicker books. Ready-made books are also handy to add to a scrapbook page for journaling, photos or memorabilia.

Debbie's "Bitty Books" are works of art in miniature. Piecing together tiny pictures, words, charms, or other notions can be a fun way to convey the gist of something or someone, be it a love note, anniversary memory, or just a friendly hello.

HOW TO

For a basic "bitty book," cut a strip 1 1/2" wide from a sheet of card stock and accordion fold it in 1" lengths, giving 11 pages. You can glue contrasting card stock on each end for covers, cutting them 1/16" to 1/8" larger than the pages. Or make a complete binding by cutting a piece of card stock 1 5/8" x 2 5/8" and scoring it to fold with a spine about 3/8" wide. You can add a sturdy spine of thin balsa wood (try looking in the doll house supplies at a craft store for small pieces). Or try a wrap-around cover that covers the entire book.

For closures, thread 1/8" ribbon in between the cover and pages with a few inches to spare on both sides. Thread a bead on both ribbons and tie the ends of the ribbons tightly so they won't fray. Cinch the bead up to the book to close it snugly. Or wrap ribbon, waxed linen, or elastic thread around the book and secure with beads or charms. These books are a perfect size to put in small boxes of any kind.

HOW TO

A photo holder is a handy solution when you have a lot of photos. For this holder I trimmed off the scalloped edge and cut the corners at an angle. Reinforce the spot for the snap by adding a small circle of paper to the back side of the snap. Assemble snap as directed. To "age" the book, rub a medium light brown ink pad across the edges.

A travel journal is great to keep in your purse on vacation to jot down the events of each day. It's nice to have a reference for sorting and journaling when photos come back from the trip.

bitty books
BY DEBBIE CROUSE
Small circle punch: Family Treasures
Rectangle punch: Paper Shapers
Mini rubber band: Silver Crow Creations
Elastic cord, wood bead: Darice
Balsa wood binding: Pearl Arts
Fiber, bead, charms: Designs by Pamela
Eyelets: Creative Impressions
Mini tag: American Tag
Ribbon: Offray

destination: england
BY ROBIN JOHNSON
Patterned paper: Autumn Leaves
Die cuts: Fresh Cuts, EK Success
Linen: Hillcreek Designs
Alphabet stamps: Personal Stamp Ex.
Block alphabet stamps: Stampers Anon.
Photo holder: Creative Memories
Spiral bound book: DMD Industries
Ink: Tsukineko
Snap: Dritz

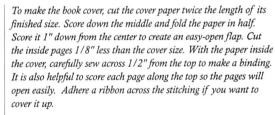

To make the book cover, cut the cover paper twice the length of its finished size. Score down the middle and fold the paper in half. Score it 1" down from the center to create an easy-open flap. Cut the inside pages 1/8" less than the cover size. With the paper inside the cover, carefully sew across 1/2" from the top to make a binding. It is also helpful to score each page along the top so the pages will open easily. Adhere a ribbon across the stitching if you want to cover it up.

odyssey

BY HEIDI SWAPP
Accordian Album:
Books by Hand
Snowflake clip: Doodles
Snowflakes, Design Ideas
Star Brads: Memory Lane
Thermometer: Memory Lane
Stamp: Personal Stamp Ex.
Embossing Powder: Suze
Weinberg Ultra Thick
Silver Paper: Black Ink
Photo Corners: Canson
Foam Core: Michael's
Grommets: Dritz
Ink: Tsukineko

See the instructions in the foam core chapter for steps on working with the foam core. Reinforce the backing with chip board, to support the weight of the accordian book. Set extra large grommets in the backing for support of the book. Run hemp around the book through the grommets to hold the book closed. Emboss over the photo with Suze Weinberg's Ultra Thick Embossing powder.

The bonus with studs and foam core is that you just stick them in and go! There is no need to bend them back.

touched by an angel

BY ROBIN JOHNSON
Printed paper: Autumn Leaves
Pencil Chalks: Pixie Press
Pens: Zig, Sakura
Ribbon: Offray

Touched by an

Angel

14 sequins

Sparkly, flashy fun is a snap with sequins. You can add zest to a page with some soft sequined accents , or you could go all out for a bright eye-catching look if you really want to!

Sequins have a way of dressing up clothes, so it's fun to take the same attitude with scrapbook pages, cards, or other crafts. Adhere them directly on the paper, or string them on wire, thread, or even a ribbon.

Notice how on "Born Beautiful," Heidi adhered sequins to photo corners rather than on the photos themselves. On Debbie's "Purely Pink" card, thin wire holds sequins in a charming curled shape.

squeaky clean
BY HEIDI SWAPP
Pencils: Prismacolor
Glitter : Magic Scraps
Letter stamps: Pixie Alphabet
Ink: Ancient Page
Hair clips: Target

purely pink
BY DEBBIE CROUSE
Die cut: Ellison
Beading wire: Darice
Sequins: Sulyn Industries
Beads: Designs by Pamela

HOW TO
Die cut the card. Trim a paint sample card to fit in the window and adhere to inside of card. Wrap beading wire around a stylus, adding beads and sequins as you go. Pierce two holes at the two ends of the window and secure the wire.

HOW TO
Look for fasteners in unexpected places: these hair clips are decorated with beads and sequins, making a perfect accent for baby pictures and word strips.

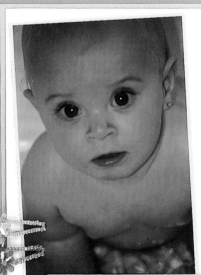

january 2 0 0 2

splish splash

quincy loves to take baths! she stands next to the edge as the water runs and laughs and bounces! then she kicks and screams in protest when it's time to get out!

8 months

Our story
isn't about a
fairy tale
princess

Ours is
better...

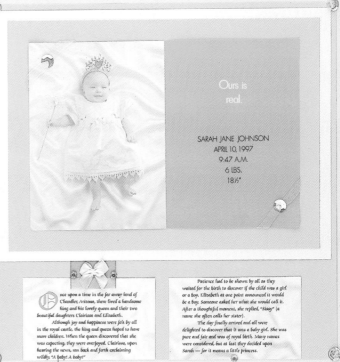

Ours is
real.

SARAH JANE JOHNSON
APRIL 10, 1997
9:47 A.M.
6 LBS.
18½"

Once upon a time in the far away land of Chandler, Arizona, there lived a handsome king and his lovely queen and their two beautiful daughters Clairissa and Elizabeth.

Although joy and happiness were felt by all in the royal castle, the king and queen hoped to have more children. When the queen discovered that she was expecting, they were overjoyed. Clairissa, upon hearing the news, ran back and forth exclaiming wildly, "A baby! A baby!"

Patience had to be shown by all as they waited for the birth to discover if the child was a girl or a boy. Elizabeth at one point announced it would be a boy. Someone asked her what she would call it. After a thoughtful moment, she replied, "Sissy" (a name she often calls her sister).

The day finally arrived and all were delighted to discover that it was a baby girl. She was pure and fair and was of royal birth. Many names were considered, but at last they decided upon Sarah — for it means a little princess.

sarah's birth announcement
BY ROBIN JOHNSON
Vellum: Autumn Leaves
Ribbon: Offray
Sequins: Bits & Pieces, Cousin Corp.
Adhesive: Glue Dots
Beads: Mill Hill

born beautiful
BY HEIDI SWAPP
Card stock: Memory Lane
Tulle ribbon: Ben Franklin
Pens: Zig Platinum
Pencils: Prismacolor
Sequins: Westrim Crafts
Photo corners: Canson

HOW TO

Iridescent sequins add just a touch of sparkle to match the jewels illustrated on these pages. The small items, such as the beads, are easy to adhere with glue dots.

HOW TO

Tulle makes an elegant pocket to hold items on the page. It's so transparent it adds only a slight texture to photos or journaling. Simply sew it to the page on three sides and slide items in.

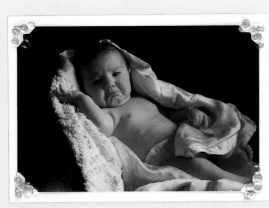

15 tags

As you've seen on other pages, we love tags! There are so many shapes and sizes of ready-made tags available, and they can add to photos, journaling, and titles - or just about anything else that needs to be identified or commented on.

Tags can be attached with string, slipped into pockets, or clipped onto photos or pages. They give you versatility with your placement of word strips or journaling blocks.

Apart from scrapbook pages, custom tags are perfect for gifts, to tack on bulletin boards, or to make gift books. Debbie's tag book has examples of just about every use for a tag, such as notes, photo holders, and even photos cut in tag shapes.

stitched tags
BY DEBBIE CROUSE
Tags: American Tag
Shadow ink: Hero Arts
Embossing powder:
Stamp-n-Stuff

holding hearts & hands
BY ROBIN JOHNSON
Ribbon: India House Ribbons
Gold thread: DMC
Beads: Mill Hill
Fabric: Benartex
Stamp: Personal Stamp Exchange
Embossing powder: Stamp-n-Stuff
Fonts: Petras & Goudy
Waxed linen: Darice
Ink: Tsukineko
Eyelet: Dritz

HOW TO

To make the embossed matte, rub gold ink pad over corners and randomly across the matte. Sprinkle embossing powder over entire area, shake off excess powder and heat set.

I printed the red title block on a single piece of card stock, leaving 3" spaces for the tags.

The three name tags are in a ribbon holder. Tape the ends of the ribbon to the page, then stitch three pockets with gold thread. Remove tape.

HOW TO

If you are lucky enough to have an embroidery machine, these are fun to make for many uses. Tape the edges of the tag to the stabilizer in the hoop. Stitch names, initials, or designs, and add buttons, tassels, or other notions.

I stamped the tags with shadow ink to give an aged appearance. The "L" tag was heat embossed on the edges.

MOM & DAD SPRANG FOR US TO TOUR KAUAI BY AIR ON OUR LAST DAY... AMAZING! THE ISLAND WAS SO DIVERSE AND SPECTACULAR...

HELI-TOUR

canyons

waterfalls

mountains

taro fields

Crater

Ocean

These handmade tags are simple card stock rectangles with the top corners cut off. Punch out 5/8" paper circles and glue to tag, then use a 1/4" punch inside the circles.

The hemp twine lays flat if you tie a square knot (right over left, then left over right).

tag book
BY DEBBIE CROUSE
Die cuts: Ellison, Accu-Cut
Stamps: Personal Stamp Ex.
Tags: American Tag
Clips: Clipiola
Binding post: Ink It!
Pins: Dritz
Studs: American Tag
Eyelets: Creative Impressions
Glue: E6000

helitour
BY HEIDI SWAPP
Square punch: Marvy
Hemp twine: Craftmart
Pencils: Prismacolor
Stamps: Personal
Stamp Exchange
Ink: Color Box
Pens: Zig

For this book I used ready-made tags and die cut others from paper and photos. I cut some with folded paper, placing the fold next to one edge so the tag can open up double-sized.

16 fibers

Fibers are sold in such interesting combinations of color and texture, you can find dozens of uses for a single package of varied fibers. They're a great way to add the unexpected to scrapbooks and crafts.

Fibers are fun to work with because they're so soft and pliable. It's easy to work them into different shapes. Twist fibers together, fray them for a lighter look, braid them, or tie them around any elements on your pages.

As simple accents, you can adhere fibers directly to paper by lightly gluing them. Or, as seen on this and other pages, tie them around pictures, frames, journaling blocks, or tags.

HOW TO — Tear a heart shape from card stock. Cut small slits around the edge to hold fibers in place. Wrap a variety of fibers across the heart, and tape ends on back to secure. Add brads where fibers cross.

All the fibers on this page came in a single package with varied colors and styles that work together so well.

HOW TO — To make the sheep, roll a small amount of fiber in your hand and tie floss around it to form a neck. Adhere to card and draw legs. Add stamped message.

I can't resist playing with words. You might also try messages like "It's all about ewe," "Ewe are special," or "I need ewe."

happy birthday two ewe
BY DEBBIE CROUSE
Embroidery floss: DMC
Letter stamps: Personal Stamp Exchange,
Wool fiber: Michael's

wanted
BY ROBIN JOHNSON
Frame: Autumn Leaves
Letter stamps: Personal Stamp Exchange
Stampers Anonymous
Fibers: K1C2, Adornaments
Ink: Tsukineko
Brads: Dritz

new niece
BY HEIDI SWAPP
Paper: Autumn Leaves
Fibers: K1C2, Adornaments
Stamp: Personal Stamp Exchange
Photo sleeve holder: Kolo
Slide holder: Impress
Magnets: Fridge Fun
Glassine envelope: Impress
Ribbon: Midori

tri-hearts card
BY DEBBIE CROUSE
Heart punch: Emaginations
Square punch: Family Treasures
Fibers: K1C2, Adornaments
Pop-up dots: Cut It Up
Thin metal: Michael's
Wire mesh: Michael's
Pin: Dritz

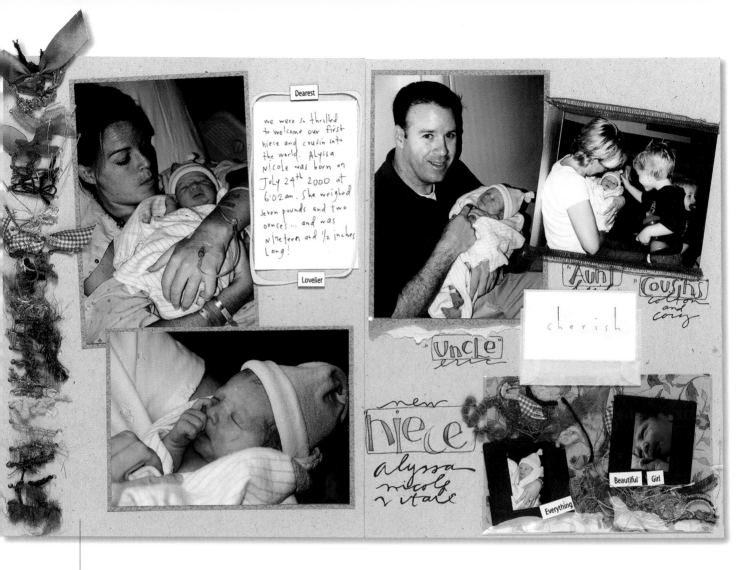

Dearest

we were so thrilled to welcome our first niece and cousin into the world. ALyssa Nicole was born on July 24th 2000 at 6:02am. She weighed seven pounds and two ounces ... and was nineteen and 1/2 inches Long!

Lovelier

Aunt

Cousins
colton and cory

cherish

"Uncle"
Eric

new
niece
alyssa
nicole
vitale

Beautiful Girl

Everything

HOW TO

To make a fiber border, use a 1/8" punch and punch two holes that are varied in their distance apart, all down the side of the page. Tie a different kind of fiber in each set of holes. You can also use ribbon and different types of strings. Also use a Kolo photo holder to hold extra fiber clippings and small photos.

HOW TO

Punch squares of color out of paint sample cards. Adhere to card with pop-up dots for a three-dimensional look. Then adhere hearts to color squares.

pins

Straight pins, safety pins, bobby pins, hat pins - there are so many possibilities for securing papers and photos together. Look for decorative pins of all kinds in your favorite craft store, and you'll find plenty of inspiration that goes beyond the obvious.

Pins can tie, tuck, and hold together parts of a page. They're good for holding items that are transparent and might show an adhesive underneath, such as vellum.

Who would think that bobby pins would be so handy for scrapbooking? Heidi's "Sledding" page uses ordinary bobby pins with letter beads glued on. They hold photos and journaling strips in place and look great with the black and white photos.

H O W T O

It's easy to print out a sheet full of sentiments, then clip and pin to a card as needed. Glue glass beads directly on card. For heart necklace, pierce two holes and pull gold elastic thread through, string the bead, pull thread through the back and tie.

For the flower, glue the leaf and flower beads and draw a stem and grass with a fine pen.

pin-ups
BY DEBBIE CROUSE
Pen: Micron
Pins: Dritz
Gold elastic thread: DMC
Glass beads & crystals: Mill Hill
Adhesive: Aleene's thick tacky glue

H O W T O

Safety pins seemed right for a toddler in diapers, especially when his backside is as fun to remember as his front!

For edges and mattes, tear a dark green piece of card stock (12" square) into long strips, then place strips on black and light green pages the same size. Run a zig-zag stitch along the torn edges. Place photos over the patchwork page and cut rectangles for mattes. Use scraps for a journaling block and for edges.

baby in motion
BY ROBIN JOHNSON
Safety pins: Dritz
Twine: Twistel, Making Memories
Fonts: Courier, various fonts for "motion"
Tags: American Tag
Ink: Shadow Ink, Hero Arts

december 2001
salt lake city

COLD

FAST

we purchashed snow boots from
R.e.I. just so we could go
sledding. the boys had the best
time, I couldn't believe how
many times they went up &
down! such fun winter memories!

SNOW

SLED

BRR

sledding

BY HEIDI SWAPP

Handmade paper: Memory Lane
Square punch: Emaginations
Snowflake sequins: Westrim
Bobby pins: Target
Letter beads: Michael's
Adhesive: E6000

HOW TO

Almost anything can be adhered to bobby pins: beads, ribbon, buttons, sequins, even photos. I used E6000 glue to attach the letter beads to the pins. Do your page layout first, then decide where to place the pins. As you add letters to make words, make sure you align the letters in the right direction depending on whether the pin will be horizontal or vertical.

pin cushion cards

BY DEBBIE CROUSE

Ribbon: Midori, Offray
Beads: Designs by Pamela
Drop pins: Darice
Corsage Pins: Dritz
Fabric: Old Scraps
Batting: Warm and Natural

HOW TO

To make a pin cushion card, cut a piece of fabric batting and cover with fabric, or leave plain. Stitch to the card. To decorate the pins, add on beads and then twist the pin in a loop to hold the beads in place. Add sentiments and pin into the batting. Decorate with ribbon or extra pins.

HAPPY BIRTHDAY

THANKS

BEST WISHES

Love you...

18 metallics

Metal objects may not seem an obvious choice for scrapbooking, but you'll be surprised how many odds and ends you can come up with that are just right for some pages. The weight and thickness of a metal object are your only limitations: you may need a sturdy chipboard or matte board if the item is too heavy to adhere to card stock. You'll likely need a sturdy adhesive as well, like E6000 or Glue Dots.

There are plenty of lightweight, flexible metal products that can be handled like paper. As shown on Robin's "Baby of Mine," you can cut metal sheets to size and use punches on them. You'll also find many pre-cut metal shapes on the market, from rusty old metal to tin, foil, and thin metal in various colors and textures.

HOW TO *I had to make over 100 invitations, so I had to think simple. Cards are printed three to a sheet and Z-folded in thirds so the printing is on one side of the paper. Small leaves are punched out of 36 gauge copper tooling foil and attached with E6000 glue. Before cutting the sheets, score the two folds (one on the front, one on the reverse) to make a neater fold. The cards are slipped into the envelopes and closed with a simple ribbon tied in a bow.*

HOW TO *Score chipboard and fold approximately in thirds, then stitch down the inside flap to form a pocket for the card. Attach container lid to metal rim tag, and tie the tag to the card. This container is perfect to hold little memory objects: flowers, sand and shells, or little pebbles, for example.*

live your dreams
BY ROBIN JOHNSON
Sticker: Mrs. Grossman's
Mesh & Metal: Michael's
Fonts: Typist, Andale
Adhesive: Glue Dots
Square Punch: Family
Treasures
Clips: Clipiola

bloomers card
BY DEBBIE CROUSE
Watercolor paper: Strathmore
Pressed flower: Pearl Arts
Hemp cord: Darice
Tag: American Tag
Aluminum container:
Memory Lane
Adhesive: E6000 glue

small things
BY DEBBIE CROUSE
Leaf punches: Family Treasures
Ribbon: Berwick Industries
Copper foil: Ben Franklin's
Glassine envelopes:
Memory Lane
Adhesive: E6000 glue
Paper trimmer/scorer: Fiskar's

february 2002

tEACH
Me To
Walk

You are practically begging to walk!
Anytime anyone will hold your hands,
you trot delightfully wherever they lead
you, and for as long as they are willing!
As for me, i selfishly want to hold
you back from growing so fast. i love
watching you crawl off behind your
brothers, as fast as your knees will
carry you, that adorable swivel of your
padded bottom. Yet i know, Nothing will
keep you from learning and growing...i
feel sad until i see that smile and
laughter of delight you get as you
achieve your milestones!

little
details!

my
dAUGHTER

teach me to walk

BY HEIDI SWAPP

Punch (1/8"): Fiskars
Metal frame: Impress
Ribbon: Bucilla
Pens: Zig Millennium
Eyelets: Impress
Suede paper: Nag Posh

Glassine envelopes: Impress
Metal corners: Boutique Trims Inc.
Pewter heart: Sundance Catalog
Fibers: Rubba Dub Dub
Patterned paper: Anna Griffin

baby of mine

BY ROBIN JOHNSON

Square punch: Family Treasures
Adhesive: Glue dots
Sheet metal: Michael's
Metal Hearts : Provo Craft
Wire: Artistic Wire
Pens: Zig

HOW TO

To add fibers, punch holes and add eyelets at the top and bottom of the page. Thread 3-4 strands through each eyelet at the top and loosely braid them down, then thread through the bottom eyelets and tie off behind.

HOW TO

The metal and punched metal shapes can be adhered with glue dots. For the decorative wire, pierce holes in the paper with a needle and thread wire through. On back of paper, bend wire flat and tape to secure.

I love
devin

devin wasn't the
only one lucky
enough to be
like grandpa

cousin jacob has
grandpa's looks
too!

devin and
grandpa
JULY
2001

Baby of mine...
where did you get eyes so blue?
grandpa maryon ... that's who
and what of your hair - blonde & fair?
grandpa maryon ... that is where
what of your sweet spirit we all love?
grandpa maryon ... and God above.

19 miniatures

Once you start working with miniatures, it's hard to stop. You'll find many styles and kinds of miniature objects in different sections of craft stores. It can be fun to build up a collection for use on scrapbook pages or other craft projects.

It's also a challenge to make your own, such as the tiny diapers Heidi made for her "Twins" page. Simple shapes and basic materials can make as little objects. And as you get hooked on charming, small proportions, you'll see connections between everyday objects, such as the hank of twine Robin used for cowboy rope.

Try highlighting a series of miniatures with a repeated design, such as the tags lined up on "A Day in the Life." This can be an effective page layout technique to give the viewer a variety of visual treats.

a day in the life
BY ROBIN JOHNSON
Hemp: Craftmart
Twine: Hillcreek Designs
Alphabet: Personal Stamp
Exchange
Ink: Tsukineko
Flour bag: Darice
Hat buttons: Dress It Up
Cowboy boot: Joshua's
Horseshoe: Provo Craft
Clothespins: Forster
Large eyelets: Dritz
Small eyelets: Magic Scraps
Cardstock: The Robin's Nest

pencil mini-book
BY DEBBIE CROUSE
Fiber: Magic Scraps
Pencil: Coffee Break Designs
Tag: American Tag
Rubber bands: Silver
Crow Creations
Glass heart: Mill Hill

twins
BY HEIDI SWAPP
Pens: Zig Millennium
Safety pins: Dritz
Scrabble letters: Tiny
Letters

HOW TO *Cut the cover card stock and inside text paper. Fold in half and punch 1/8" holes along the fold. Thread rubber bands through holes and around the pencil to make a binding. Tie fiber around the outside as a closure and tie on a tag.*

HOW TO *To "burn" the edges of the paper, tear it and then rub with black chalk. The tags are hand-cut rectangles with the corners trimmed. Large eyelets are added and twine threaded through the eyelets.*

Objects with dimension can be hard to glue. My pick for adhesive is to use Glue Dots.

This page is done with a regular page protector on one side, and a fold-out page protector on the other side so I have 3 panels.

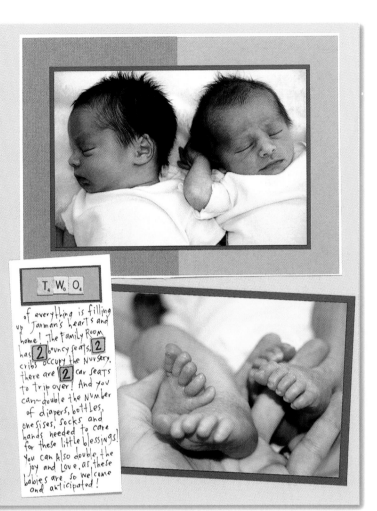

T₂ W₀ O₄

of everything is filling up Jarman's hearts and home! The Family Room has 2 bouncy seats, 2 cribs occupy the Nursery, there are 2 car seats to trip over! And you can... double the Number of diapers, bottles, onesises, socks and hands needed to care for these little blessings! You can Also double the joy and love, as these babies are so welcome and anticipated!

HOW TO

Cut the mini-diapers out of real diaper cloth or cheese-cloth. First, cut out cloth in the shape of an anvil. Fold in half lengthwise, then fold over the pointed ends toward the middle and secure with a tiny safety pin.

HOW TO

For the title, use an embroidery machine to stitch the word "Journey" on fabric. Add light padding behind and fasten to the book cover with studs. Attach the miniature bottle to the book binding with string and tie a ribbon around it. The bottle can be filled with sand from the beach or other tiny objects from your journey.

da boss

looking for their next volunteer

journey travel journal
BY DEBBIE CROUSE
Journal: Diane's
Studs: Dritz
Bottle: Darice
Ribbon: Offray

20 studs & brads

Tiny metal studs and brads have come a long way since the basic brass brads we remember from grade school. You can now find them in various colors, sizes, and styles. They're perfect for fastening together all kinds of papers and accents.

When working with studs, be careful not to bend or crease the paper. It's helpful to position the stud, tap lightly with a hammer to set the holes in place, then carefully push the stud through.

HOW TO

Cut card stock into 1 1/4" strips, sprinkle on clear embossing powder, and heat set it. Cut into different lengths and place around edges to form a frame. Emboss the heads of the studs with white embossing powder. Using two studs per intersection, fasten the strips together to form the frame. Adhere the frame to the page. After the frame is assembled, retouch the embossing by reheating to smooth out any cracks made while putting the page together.

Make the photo corners by cutting squares out of extra embossed strips, then cutting diagonally into triangles.

HOW TO

This prom invitation has the name of the sender scrambled on squares made with a sticky-back magnet sheet. Attach the metal plate to the card with brads. Print the message and name and stick the paper to the magnetic sheet. Cut out the message in a word strip. Cut squares with the letters of the sender's name and scatter around the metal plate.

HOW TO

Attach a square of wire screen to the card with brads. Stamp the message to card stock and slide behind the screen. Other tags and items are attached to the screen with pins, wire, and waxed linen.

HOW TO

Position photo where you would like it on the matte. Next, add ribbon across the photo. For the holly accents, run the vellum die-cut leaves through a Xyron machine and add to page. Punch small holes where you want the red brad "berries" to be, and insert them. To raise center photo, put foam core or matte board behind white paper. To color the tag, press several metallic ink pads (bronze, gold) onto it until covered with desired amount of ink and tie tag on with a ribbon.

how about prom?
BY DEBBIE CROUSE
Glossy card stock: Xpedx
Ribbon: Offray
Brads: American Tag
Metal plate: Home Depot
Magnetic sheet: Michael's

christmas magic
BY ROBIN JOHNSON
Red Brads: Magic Scraps
Paper: Black Ink
Die-cuts: Pixie Press
Tag: American Tag
Gold Ribbon: Offray
Green ribbon: Bucilla

missing you
BY DEBBIE CROUSE
Tags: Ellison
Ink pad: Memories
Letter stamps: Personal
Stamp Exchange
Brads: American Tag
Wire: Darice
Pins: Dritz

2000 holiday season
BY HEIDI SWAPP
Card stock: Bazzill Basics
Font: Garamouche by P22
Ink: India Ink
Letter stamps: PSX Antique
Stamp pad: Colorbox
Embossing enamel: Suze
Wineburg Ultra Thick Powder
Studs: Magic Scraps
Raffia: Coloraffia

amour mini-book
BY HEIDI SWAPP
Printed paper: Autumn Leaves
Leaf: Black Ink
Tags: American Tag
Round brad: Magic Scraps
Star brad: Memory Lane
Embossing powder: Suze
Weinburg Ultra Thick
Twine: Hobby Lobby
Fiber: Magic Scraps
Letter stamps: Personal
Stamp Exchange
Metal frame: Memory Lane
Clip: Clipiola

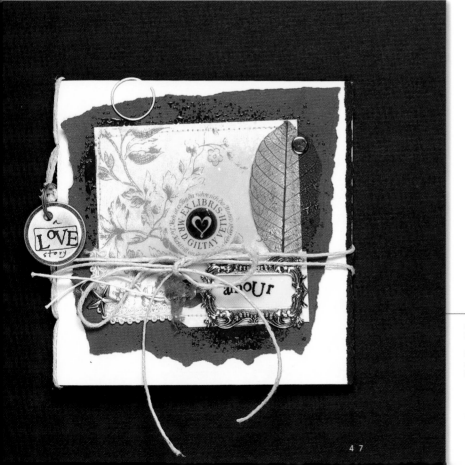

HOW TO

This handmade book has an ornate cover with several layers built up. Place torn red vellum, printed paper, leaf, tag, and fabric edging in place and sew onto cover. Sprinkle embossing powder over these layers and heat set it. Add clip, keychain tag, and metal frame, and tie book closed with twine.

21 eyelets

Metal eyelets are so versatile in crafts and scrapbooks: they can tie frames together, hold captions or titles in place, and provide strong holes for things to tie, such as ribbons or cords. Robin's "A Life Full of Firsts" shows examples of all these techniques.

With the right tools, eyelets are easy to add. Use an eyelet mat or other flexible surface to work on. Begin by punching a hole with an anywhere punch. Insert the eyelet in the hole with the tube (straight) end of the eyelet on the back of the paper. Placing the paper face down, hold the eyelet setter over the tube end and tap firmly a few times with a craft hammer. Remove the setter and give one more firm tap with the hammer to finish flattening the eyelet.

my funny valentines
BY ROBIN JOHNSON
Heart-shaped eyelets: Creative Impressions
Round eyelets: Magic Scraps
Paper: Robin's Nest
Corrugated cardboard: DMD Industries
Embossing powder: Stampendous
Silver ties: American Tag
Stamp: Provo Craft
Micro beads: Beedz
Adhesive: Magic Scraps
Font: McGarey
Ink: Tsukineko

welcome home & look cards
BY DEBBIE CROUSE
Eyelets: Dritz and Creative Impressions
Eyes: Darice
Alphabet stamps: Printworks, Personal Stamp Exchange

a life full of firsts
BY ROBIN JOHNSON
Photographer: Tim Collins
Patterned paper: Sei
Buttons: Hillcreek Designs
Fonts: Little Days, Am. Typewriter
Small eyelets: Creative Impressions
Large eyelets: Dritz
Ribbon: Offray

See Resources Section page 63

HOW TO
Print or copy the sentiment on card stock, leaving spaces for eyelets. Punch holes for eyelets with an anywhere punch, and apply eyelets. The "Look" card has rubber-stamped letters and plastic puppet eyes glued on the inside of the card.

HOW TO
Heart-shaped eyelets were perfect for this page. The silver tag ties come with a ball on the end that is just larger than the eyelet hole.

The heart in the lower right corner is made with Beedz, tiny glass beads without holes that can be adhered for a glittery look. Simply cut or punch out the shape that you want in a sheet of adhesive (or you can use tape and use it for a border or matte). Pour the beads over the adhesive shape and press down on beads. Shake excess beads back into the jar.

my funny valentines

crissy   lizzie

giving dad's car a heart attack

the girls and i had so much fun decorating daddy's car! the streamers, the homemade hearts, and 2 giggly girls filled our Valentines day with love & memories.

valentine's day   february 1997

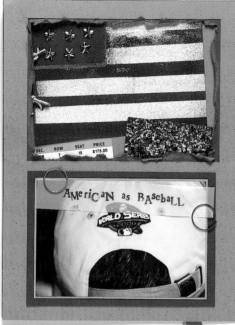

american as baseball

BY HEIDI SWAPP

Square punch: Family Treasures
Embroidery floss: DMC
Hemp twine: Michael's
Pens: Zig, EK Success
Chalks: Pixie Press
Letter stamps: PSX

Ink: Ancient Page "Coal"
Eyelets: Magic Scraps
Key tags, jewelry tags:
American Tag
Star studs: Memory Lane
Slide holder: Impressions
Flag: Made by a friend

To add double eyelets, just insert the smaller eyelet into the larger and set both at the same time.

I made a fold-down half page on the left by trimming a page protector and sewing it to the bottom of the page. The slide holder contains photo details that were punched with a 2" square punch; captions are added on jewelry tags. The flag "pole" is a bamboo skewer, inserted through two holes punched on the page.

HOW TO

---

first
boy

a life full of **firsts**

first
son

first
baby

first
nephew

When PETER entered our lives, there was something wonderful and new about each day. My friend had always told me, "there's **nothing like a first baby.**" I have realized how true it is! With Peter, everything is a first, and it will never be that way again.

peter collins
2 weeks old

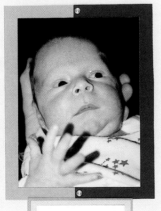

first
miracle

first
grandson

22 frames

Scrapbook pages are all about framing photos, so why not bring actual photo frames into the picture? It's easy to find flat or miniature frames that can be adhered to card stock or a heavier board.

If you have a thicker frame you can't resist using, try setting it into a foam core backing. On Heidi's "Four," a foam core cover page for an album holds both a metal frame and a smaller handmade book.

kylie
BY HEIDI SWAPP
Paper: Anna Griffin
Ribbon: Midori, Bucilla
Frame: Hobby Lobby
Font: Garamouche

family quote book
BY DEBBIE CROUSE
Frames: Memory Lane
Ribbon: Offray
Eyelet: Dritz
Letter beads: Bits & Pieces
Elastic cord: JoAnn's
Letter stamps: Hero Arts
Sandalwood: Ancient Page
Adhesive: Aleene's Thick Tacky glue
Toggle clasp: Beads Galore Int.
Journal: Silkbooks by World Paper
Button: Old Collection
Embossing powder: Suze
Weinberg's Ultra Thick

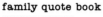

HOW TO

For the little frame with the family name, stamp the name on card stock and let dry. Emboss with at least two coats of ultra thick embossing powder and heat set. Roll the embossed paper back and forth to make small cracks, then rub a brown ink pad against it, working ink into the cracks to give it an aged look.

Glue all elements onto the journal cover except the frame on the elastic cord. On the back cover, punch a hole 1/2" from the left and set an eyelet in it. Thread elastic cord through the frame, and thread the ends of the cord through the eyelet and attach inside the book.

HOW TO

This simple page is striking, with close-up photos to catch the eye and a metal frame as a centerpiece. Simply break off the frame backing and remove the glass to use the frame. Adhere with something strong, like thick glue dots.

Kylie is about the Cutest, sweetest 11-year-old that I have ever had the pleasure of meeting. She always has a Smile on her face and is willing to help you out in aNy way! she is loves her friends, little kids and doing anything outside. She's the best big sister ever! (and she puts up with JAKE!)

H O W T O

I removed the glass and back of the picture frame and cut a rectangle out of the foam core just large enough to hold it in place.

For the handmade book I used white ink with a quill pen to write on the black paper. The book is held in place with hemp twine threaded through eyelets to the back of the page.

H O W T O

The "before and after" comparison on this page is set off with the tiny frames that hold the young children's photos next to the current photos. The family portrait on the right is set up off the page with foam core and accented with metal corner pieces. A paper matte completes the frame with a minimum of work.

blink of an eye
BY ROBIN JOHNSON
Paper: Anna Griffin
Pen: Zig, EK Success
Sheet metal: Michael's
Corner punch: Emagination
Metal corners: Boutique Trims Inc.
Metal frames: Memory Lane
Foam core: Michael's
Fibers: Adornaments
Font: Eros
Studs: Dritz

four
BY HEIDI SWAPP
Frame: Michael's
Letter stamps: PSX Antique
Ink: Encre Blanche
Quill Pen: Craftmart
Tags: American Tag
Linen: Fabric Scraps
Hemp and foam core:
Michael's

See Resources Section page 63

23 hinges

Small metal hinges can invite the viewer to open a door to something new. In contrast to the simple technique of folding paper in booklet style, hinges can add a sense of permanence, as on Heidi's "Sisterhood" page. They can also secure something of value in place, as shown on Debbie's Mother's day book (which takes the award for the most complicated project in this book!).

Hinges require a sturdy adhesive, such as E6000, or can be fastened to the paper or board with brads or wire.

sarah
BY ROBIN JOHNSON
Patterned paper: Black Ink,
MM Colors by Design
Card stock: Making Memories
Flowers: The Natural Paper Co.,
EK Success, Jolee's Boutique
Fiber: On the Surface
Eyelets: Making Memories
Hinges: Home Depot

key to my heart
BY ROBIN JOHNSON
Lock: Home Depot
Roses: Apropos
Adhesive: E6000
Foam core: Michael's
Shadow box: Target
Stamps: Personal Stamp
Exchange
Ink: Tsukineko

you hold
the key to
my heart

HOW TO

Cut a rectangle of foam core for each letter. Three of these are fastened to hinges and lift up, revealing additional journaling. The hinges are fastened to paper with brads but are simply glued to the foam core.

Eyelets help to hold the fibers in place on the bottom of the right page.

HOW TO

Cut two identical frames of foam core, and cut a piece of card stock the same size. In the shadow box, place the backing paper and adhere flowers to it. Attach the back lock clasp to one piece of foam core and adhere to the backing paper. Glue hinge to the bottom layer of foam core, then glue to the top piece of foam core. Adhere a piece of page protector over the foam core and add the card stock on top. Attach the top clasp covering the card stock and foam core.

I found this clasp on an old children's journal. It has small teeth on it so it holds itself in place without any adhesive.

life long
hero

memory

support
growth
trust

gift
sharing secrets
unconditional love
caring + true
beauty forever
understanding LOVE
laughter
friendship
strength
comfort = acceptance
sisterhood devotion
loyal
strength

kiley

Being the oldest sister is a unique position. Each new chapter of life is experienced for the first time. The oldest has to be the trailblazer and learn by trial and error. Through these learning experiences, lessons learned, valuable knowledge is gained to pass on to a younger sister.

sisterhood/friendship
BY HEIDI SWAPP
Paper: K & Co.
Ink: Encre Blanche
Clips: Clipiola
Leaves: Black Ink
Fiber: Adornaments
Photo sleeves: Kolo
Hinges: Sunburst Shutters
Trim: source unknown
Quill pen: Craftmart

HOW TO

This book looks normal from the outside, but the back half has been hollowed out to hold small photos and a "secret compartment" with a mini-book inside. A series of clues in the front part of the book lead to the treasure in the back. To create one like this, hollow out the pages with an x-acto knife and lightly glue the pages in the back of the book together. Use brads to attach the hinges to the page.

HOW TO

The hinges are placed between layers of paper so only the spines are showing. To keep the hinged photos free in a page protector, cut a slit in the page protector over the hinge so the photo and hinge are outside. Add a Kolo photo sleeve over the outside photo to protect it.

Try using a quill pen for a fluid style. I wrote in white ink on a dark cardstock for variety.

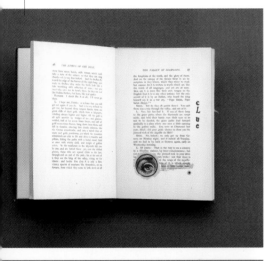

See Resources Section page 63

On this special day we're sending you a treat
From a group of those who love you, so relax and have a seat.
Turn to page twenty-four you'll find a little note
open it and inside, a message for you we wrote.

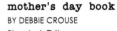

mother's day book
BY DEBBIE CROUSE
Star stud: Dritz
Brads: American Tags
Fiber: Adornaments
Ribbon: Mortex
Imagine charm: Designs by Pamela
Stamps: Personal Stamp Exchange
Inks: Printworks, Hero Arts
Clasp & hinges: Demis Products
Adhesive: Perfect Paper Adhesive

foam core

Foam core is a great, lightweight tool to add depth to scrapbook pages. You can use it as a frame around objects that are set into the page. This is especially useful if you need to protect items that are fragile (like seashells.) Or if you have a bulky item (like a lifesaver) that would not sit well on a flat page, a foam core frame will allow for it's thickness. (See examples on pages 56 and 58 for more ideas.)

Use foam core like a cork board: You can push pins or brads directly into it to hold items in place. Debbie's "Ribon Memo Card" is like a mini-memo board, and on Robin's "Conway 2001" page the gold cord is held in place with sequin pins pressed in the side of the foam core.

Foam core is also a perfect backing when you want to lift something off the page. For small items, pop-up dots or squares work great. Larger items can sometimes sag in the middle if it is only "popped-up" in spots. Using a piece of foam core gives a solid base to accentuate your piece.

ribbon memo card

BY DEBBIE CROUSE
Floral paper: Anna Griffin
Foam core: Michael's
Envelope die: Ellison
Ribbon: Renaissance
Tassle: Artifacts Inc.
Picture Pebbles: Magic Scraps

conway 2001

BY ROBIN JOHNSON
Floral paper: Anna Griffin
Card stock: Bazzill Basics
Heart square: Autumn Leaves
Foam core: Michael's
Floral stamp: PSX
Letters: Printworks
Inks: Tsukineko
Studs: Dritz
Tassles & cording:
Hirschberg Schutz & Co.
Sequin pins: Dritz

HOW TO

Cut foam core 4 1/2" by 6 1/4" with an Xacto knife and metal straight edge. Cut card stock the same size. Wrap 1 1/2 yards ribbon around both to look like a memo board. Attach messages with push pins.

This card works best with a gusseted envelope to expand for the thickness of the foam core.

HOW TO

Foam core sets off both the family portrait and the heart design on these pages. Gold cord embellishes the otherwise plain edge of the foam core, and is matched on the other page with cord tied around the heart.

family vacation:
capturing moments

BY HEIDI SWAPP

Handmade paper: Black Ink
Punch: Family Treasures
Remember stamp: Stampa Rosa
Letter stamps: PSX Classic Lowercase
Ink: Ancient Page

Key tag: American Tag
Eyelets: Magic Scraps
Elastic cord: Craftmart
Star studs: Memory Lane
Chalk Pencils: Pixie Press
Hemp twine: Michael's
Label holder: source unknown

HOW TO

The left page is made with foam core with an inset for the handmade book. Two grommets are set in the backing paper at the corners of the inset, and elastic cord is threaded through to hold the book in place.

For the "Capturing Moments" photo collage, I got an extra set of prints and went crazy with a 1 1/2" square punch. Use care in adhering the photo squares so the space between them is even on all sides.

STEP BY STEP

foam core

1 Plan your page and determine where your cut outs will be located on cardstock. Keep in mind that to fit in a page protector, you will have to trim your overall page down by 3/8" off the top and side.

2 Mark the windows with pencil and cut them out of the card stock first.

3 Lay the page on the foam core and trace the outside, and the windows with a pencil.

4 Using an exacto knife and a ruler (or straight edge), Cut the foam core along your markings. TIP: DON'T TRY TO CUT ALL THE WAY THROUGH THE FOAM BOARD IN ONE SWIPE. PLAN TO MAKE 4-5 PASSES WITH YOUR KNIFE FOR EACH CUT, CUTTING DEEPER WITH EACH PASS.

5 Cut a piece of card stock to fit the back of the foam core.

6 After you have completed your layout, glue it all together. First apply glue to the back of the foam core and position the face of your layout. If you are setting grommets in the back of your layout to secure a book, set them before you glue.

mini-books

1 Cut 12 x 12 cardstock in half and then fold in half again.

2 Punch two holes on the spine of the book for binding with hemp.

3 Each page inside the cover needs to be cut 1/8" smaller than the one before so the edge is even. So using your paper trimmer, take each "page" while folded in half, and cut 1/8" off the edge opposite the fold; then 1/4" off the next; then 3/8" off the next and so on.

4 Finish off by tying knots or doing macrame loops with the hemp.

anything goes

We hope you've been inspired by the many ideas in this book. Here are a few more projects that combine the techniques you've already seen. As you find new sewing notions, craft supplies, doo-dads, gizmos, and cute little thingys, have fun incorporating them into your scrapbooks and crafts!

lifesaver thank-you
BY HEIDI SWAPP
Key tags: American Tag
Embroidery floss: DMC
Watercolor: Nicholson's
Peerless Watercolors
Foam core: Staples

pretty in plaid stationery set
BY DEBBIE CROUSE
Vellum: Autumn Leaves
Vellum envelopes: IFR Clearing
Clear side-loading envelope: Smead
Eyelets: Dritz

the dishwasher stage
BY HEIDI SWAPP
Square punch: Marvy
Pens: Zig, EK Success
Pencils: Prismacolor
Trim: The Trim Shoppe
Photo corners: Canson
Eyelets: Creative Impressions

2002 paralympics
BY ROBIN JOHNSON
Card stock: Bazzill Basics
Embossing powder: Stampendous!
Foam core: Michael's
Stamps: Personal Stamp Exchange, Hero Arts
Inks: Color Box

HOW TO *Cut card-size pieces of foam core in a frame shape. Adhere to watercolor paper background. Cut two colors of card stock and tear an opening in both. Adhere card stock to foam core, either before or after you wrap embroidery floss around the card. Stamp sentiment on tag and tie to the floss. Lightly adhere the lifesavers in place, or enclose in a transparent envelope.*

Line the inside of a side-loading plastic envelope with sheets of vellum and cardstock, scoring as needed to make a cleaner fold. Cut strips from leftover pieces to wrap around each card. Punch a 1/8" hole through the vellum and card and tie with ribbon. Use other leftover pieces to make gift cards: cut card stock and vellum approximately 1 3/4" x 8", fold in half, punch a 1/8" hole near the fold and thread ribbon through.

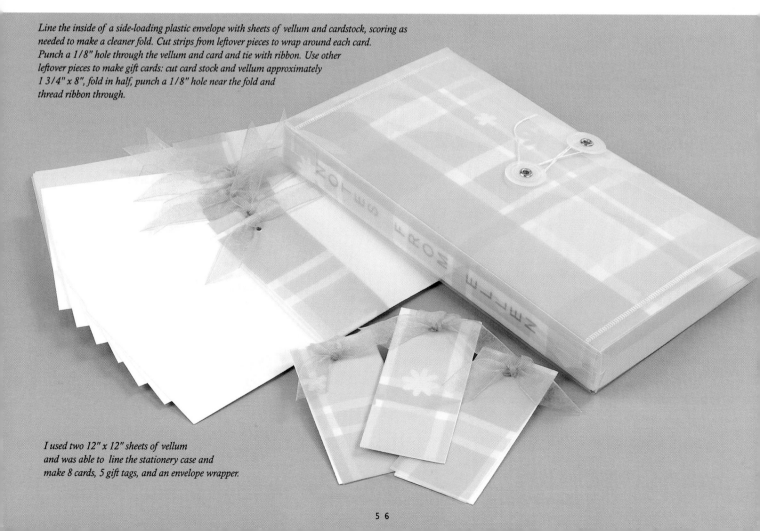

I used two 12" x 12" sheets of vellum and was able to line the stationery case and make 8 cards, 5 gift tags, and an envelope wrapper.

JANUARY '02

it happens to all of them, about the time they learn to pull up on things— it's an un-canny ability to detect the open dishwasher door! They crawl to the open door, pull up and proceed to unload it's contents, on to the floor, but not before each item goes directly into the mouth to aide in the teething process...

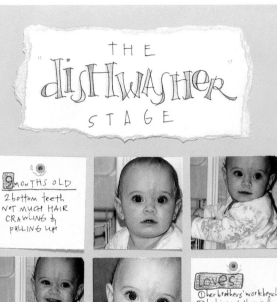

THE "DISHWASHER" STAGE

9 MONTHS OLD
2 bottom teeth
NOT MUCH HAIR
CRAWLING &
PULLING UP

LOVES
① her brothers' workbench
② looking out the window
③ her burpie
④ the dog dish
⑤ bath time

i love her dressed in PINK!
i love her sweet little voice
i love her BIG BLUE eyes!
i love her bright smile
and that she is totally
TICKELISH!

HOW TO *For the torn edges of the title block, I lightly shaded with a pencil. The trim around the photo is adhered with glue dots. The doubled eyelets are set at the same time (one inside the other) and then I give one more tap on the front to flatten them.*

HOW TO *I combined my own hand-printed and stamped words with titles and text cut from the opening ceremonies program. To make the mini-book, I cut paper to size and then had it bound at a print shop. I had a lot of thoughts and feelings I wanted to remember from the Paralympics, but I didn't have any more photos. The mini-book gave me the extra journaling room I needed.*

DREAM

ASCEND

TRiUMPH

AWAKEN THE MIND

AWAKEN THE MIND The power of the mind awakens each of us to possibilities. It ignites a passion to pursue a dream. From a child's wish to the intense focus that precedes a competition, the mind opens us to our potential.

FREE THE BODY The physicality of an athlete is the purest expression of the human form. Breaking barriers, speeding down slopes or gliding across the snow or ice, each body is a vessel that allows us to reach for greatness. Strength and endurance sweep aside physical challenges in a celebration of human achievement.

INSPIRE THE SPIRIT An invincible will leads us on a journey into the essence of the human experience. The athletes and all of humanity are guided by this enduring force—a spirit that compels us to realize our full capacity as human beings and to inspire one another.

My brother-in-law, JOHN BREWER, is a former paralympic athlete. When Salt Lake hosted the Paralympics, John got to speak, and carry the torch. Watching him and the athletes inspired me and taught me about the strength and courage of the human spirit.

FREE THE BODY

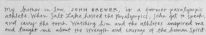

MEMORIES HOPES & dreams
inspired by the paralympics

JOURNEY of FiRE

INSPIRE THE SPIRIT

JUNE 2001

We all loved our day at Carmel Beach. What an experience!! I'm not sure what I loved the most... the gentle breeze, the sparkle on the water, the cool soft sand between my toes, the rhythmic sound of the waves, the seashell search or the joy on the children's faces... INCREDIBLE.

We're LOVIN LIFE ON THE Carmel

Beach

HOW TO

Cut foam core boxes to size with an Xacto knife. Press a stamp pad several times on the foam core to color it. You can also add embossing powder and heat set it for a glossy look. Adhere card stock slightly larger than the boxes to the backing page, then adhere the foam core and shells to the card stock.

See Resources Section page 63

survivor
BY DEBBIE CROUSE
Bottle: Western Plastics Corp.
Hemp: Darice
Sea shells: Magic Scraps

wet paint
BY DEBBIE CROUSE
Watercolor paper: Strathmore
Vellum: Paper Adventures
Paint can: Home Depot
Paint: Nicholson's Peerless
Water Colors
Pins, stud: Dritz

lovin' the beach
BY ROBIN JOHNSON
Patterned paper: Pixie Press
Vellum: Karen Foster Design
Tags: American Tag
Chalk pencils: Pixie Press
Sea shells: Magic Scraps
Foam core: Michael's
Clips: Clipiola

sweet & sour
BY HEIDI SWAPP
Vellum: Autumn Leaves
Ribbon: Memory Lane
Pens: Zig, EK Success
Pencil: Prismacolor
Buttons: Making Memories
Embroidery Floss: DMC
Tags: American Tag
Word Tags: Chronicle Books
Rectangle Punch: Family
Treasures

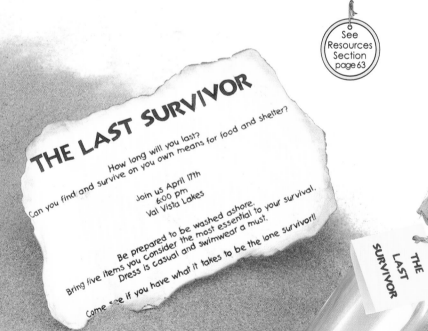

THE LAST SURVIVOR

How long will you last?
Can you find and survive on you own means for food and shelter?

Join us April 17th
6:00 pm
Val Vista Lakes

Be prepared to be washed ashore.
Bring five items you consider the most essential to your survival.
Dress is casual and swimwear a must.

Come see if you have what it takes to be the lone survivor!!

THE LAST SURVIVOR

HOW TO

For this message in a bottle, add sand and shells first. Print the message and tear the edges of the paper. Burn or rub chalk on the edges. For the lid, cut a circle of card stock, soak it in water, and gently crumple it. While still wet, wrap around bottle opening and tie with hemp twine.

Cut watercolor paper to size, paint designs on, and let dry. Fold cards and attach vellum *"wet paint"* signs with small pins. Attach printed information on the inside with a stud.

Make a set of these for a friend and deliver in a plain paint can with a custom label. They can be used as housewarming invitations or simply as change of address cards.

a few more
ideas

We hope you have enjoyed the different materials and ideas we collected and created for this book. We have had a great time as we have been inspired by some wonderful products!

Our hope is that something here will inspire you for your next creation. Don't limit yourself to re-creating the projects you see. Instead, try to remember the idea or techniques that you learn and apply it to your next page, done in your own style.

There are so many great sources for ideas, especially when it comes to notions. Books, magazines and catalogs are full of inspiring images. Notice how easily Heidi and Debbie adapted these ideas. Debbie was inspired by *Victoria* magazine, and Heidi's concept was adapted from *Beautiful Ribbons* by Mary Norden.

There is inspiration in the world around us. Incorporate your ideas with the new techniques you've learned here and enjoy experimenting with the wonderful world of notions.

get well flowers
BY DEBBIE CROUSE
Vial: from florist
Raffia: Coloraffia
Embroidery floss: DMC
Stamps: Personal
Stamp Exchange

"I always thought it would be fun to have fresh flowers on a card. With a vial, you can do it! Just attach the vial to the card."

baby blues
BY HEIDI SWAPP
Paper: Memory Lane
Punch:
Stamps: Personal
Stamp Exchange
Ribbon: Midori, Offray,
Eyelets: Magic Scraps
Metal holder:

about the artists

robin

Robin Johnson lives in Farmington, Utah with her husband, Andrew and her four children: Crissy, Lizzie, Sarah and Devin. She has a degree in Graphic Design and has been a scrapbooker for nine years. She has enjoyed teaching classes across the country and at CKU. She is a Creating Keepsakes' 2000 Hall of Fame winner, and the creator of several products, including her first book, "Designing with Vellum."

Robin loves time with her husband, children, siblings and friends. She is always up late working on projects and so her studio is named Starlit Studio. If she had any spare time, she would enjoy playing tennis, playing the piano or eating Krispy Kreme donuts with a friend.

debbie

Debbie Crouse grew up in Phoenix, Arizona. She attended Phoenix College majoring in fashion merchandising. Debbie discovered her love for paper arts while working at Memory Lane scrapbooking store. There she has taught classes and helps with creative work whenever she can. Debbie was a major contributor in Autumn Leaves' first book, "Designing with Vellum."

Debbie and her husband Skip have four children and two grandchildren. Her son, Jared, and his wife, Kathy, are the parents of her grandsons, Cole and Will. She has a daughter, Emali, and two more sons, Skyler and Logan. Debbie keeps busy with all her children's sports and music activities and helps with the youth programs in her church.

heidi

Heidi Swapp lives in Mesa, Arizona with her husband, Eric, and her three children (and subjects of her art work): Colton, Cory and Quincy. She is originally from Salk Lake City, Utah, where she attended the University of Utah seeking a degree in Exercise physiology. She has no formal artistic training, although she would love to study art and photography in the future.

Heidi has loved to scrapbook for as long as she can remember. She has developed and taught many classes for her favorite "lss", Memory Lane, in Mesa, AZ. She was recognized as one of the "25 best scrapbookers" in the Creating Keepsakes Hall of Fame in 2000. She has written articles for Creating Keepsakes and Simple Scrapbooks Magazine. She loves travel, traditions and staying up all night long to scrapbook.

author

dan

Dan Maryon lives in Orem, Utah with his wife, Dorothy, and their children Kate, Rachel, and Ethan. He is originally from Salt Lake City, where he graduated from the University of Utah with a degree in French. Dan has worked as an editor, writer, and manager for 16 years with various software companies in Utah and California.

Dan enjoys gardening, hiking, scrapbooking, and camping with his family in his spare time. He is also the author of Autumn Leaves' first book, "Designing with Vellum."

about us

Autumn Leaves began in the stationery industry six years ago. At one point, they noticed that the sales of their paper were going up, but the sales of their envelopes were going down. After some research, they discovered that the paper was being purchased by scrapbookers who, of course, didn't need the envelope! They recognized the perfect match between their beautiful papers and the scrapbookers desire to create beautiful pages. A new company was born!

Autumn Leaves began producing stickers and vellum pages - some of the most artistic and beautiful vellum on the market. They also acquired Whispers, which is a vellum line. They decided to begin publishing idea books and realized the need for an idea book all about vellum. In September of 2001, they published *Designing with Vellum* by Robin Johnson. The success was amazing and it is now in its third printing.

Designing With Notions is the second book in the "The Sophisticated Scrapbook Series." Autumn Leaves plans to continue with their papers, vellums, stickers and book series. Watch for new product releases throughout the year.

Jeff Lam is the owner and creative director for Autumn Leaves.

books

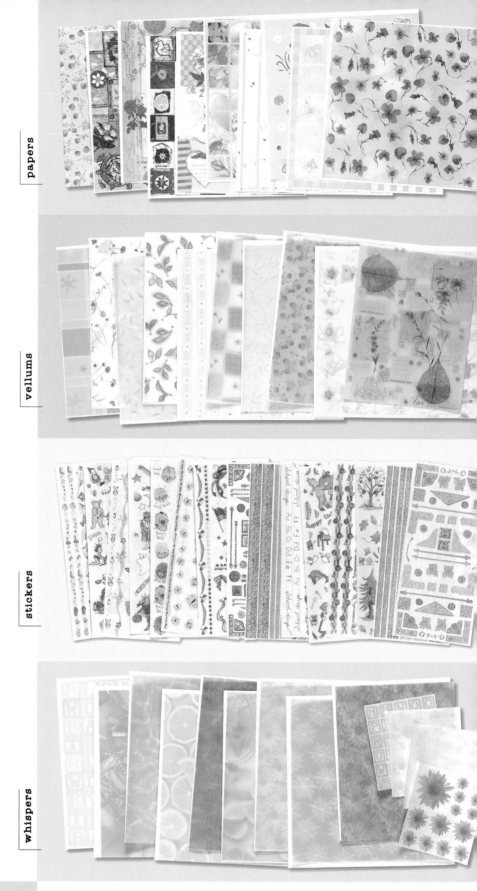

papers

vellums

stickers

whispers

Autumn Leaves
For Scrapbooking

resources

glue dots

WEB: www.gluedots.com
E-MAIL: info@gludots.com

Glue Dots International
5575 So. Westridge Drive
New Berlin, WI 53151

Glue Dots®.. the new way to glue! Fast, safe, easy to use, acid-free... no waiting for the glue to dry. Adhere buttons, charms. pressed flowers, even tiny rhinestones and bows. Glue Dots bind anything... instantly! Four products to choose from.

making memories

801.294.0430
fax 801.294.0439

P.O. Box 1188
1168 W. 500 N.
Centerville, Utah 84014

Dare to Detail!™ Are you ready to add embellishments to your pages? Just eait till you see our new shaped buttons, beads, eyelets, tags, snaps, Twistel, and wire. All packaged in easy to organize containers. Remember, it's all in the Details!™

hillcreek designs

www.hillcreekdesigns.com
10159 Buena Vista Ave.
Santee, CA 92071

Theresa's Hand Dyed buttons are available in nine sizes 5/16" (Itsy Bitsy) to 1 1/8", and 50 different colors. May be purchased in indicidual size and color packages or mixed sizes and color bags. We also offer Normandy Linen Thread that comes on 2" old fashioned wooden spools in 3 weights.

magic scraps

www.magicscraps.com
#103 Spring Creek Village
Dallas, TX 75248
Ph: (972) 385-1838
Fax: (972) 385-1407

Magic Scraps™ is your one stop source for mixed media embellishments that add a truly magical touch to paper crafts. Products include Shaved Ice,™ Craft Tinsel,™ tons of tools and lots more!

prym-dritz

www.dritz.com
P.O. Box 5028
Spartanburg, S,C.,
        29304

Our family of product includes: Dritz sewing notions (eyelets, grommets, decorative studs and more) quilting notions and other craft products.

jolee's boutique, ek success

973.458.0092 • 800.524.1349
fax 973.594.0543 • 800 767.2963

125 Entin Road
P.O. Box 1141
Clifton, NJ 07014

Jolee's Boutique, brought to you by Stickopotamus, are unique, hand-made, 3-dimensional stickers that are very intricate in detail.

black ink

800-323-1660

creative impressions

719.596.4860

tsukineko

www.tsukineko.com

american tag

800.223.3956

adornaments™ fibers, klc2

www.pattiewack.com

mill hill

www.millhill.com

dmc

www.dmc-usa.com

designs by pamela

www.designsbypamela.com

CONTACT US

autumn leaves

15821 Ventura Blvd.
Suite #565
Encino, California 91436

1.800.588.6707 or 1.818.907.5977
1.818.380.6776 (fax)

For information, contact:

Josie Kinnear [OPERATIONS MANAGER]
Alanna Arthur [PROJECTS MANAGER]
Tim Collins [MARKETING DIRECTOR]

Autumn Leaves
For Scrapbooking